30-06-01

15-00

Highland Whistle Blower

The True Story of the Phil Durham Affair

PE DURHAM

Northern Books
from Famedram

From the same author:

THE FÜHRER LED BUT WE OVERTOOK HIM
in a Captured U-boat at War

Pentland Press 1997

Published by Famedram Publishers Limited PO Box 3 AB41 9EA
Printed by Thomson Press C-35 Phase II Noida 201 305 Ref 100301

Foreword

*By Lord Campbell of Croy, P.C., M.C.** *
(formerly The Rt Hon Gordon Campbell, M.P.)

PHIL Durham's history of unusual events in the Highlands of Scotland during the 1960s provides a factual record of what actually happened and why. Resident in the area at the time, he is in a unique position to do this as one of the first employees of the Highlands and Islands Development Board who,, when he became aware ofwhat seemed to him a misuse of public funds, caused a row.

His own memory and notes have been confirmed and supplemented by official Government and Scottish Office documents released under the 30 year rule. The public, on request, can now read the correspondence and memoranda initiated in the 1960s by ministers and officials in departments and agencies. Guessing is no longer necessary. Ministers' views and the minutes of confidential meetings are now open for all to see.

Mr Durham has assiduously studied this recently available material and made use of it where it relevantly completes the picture. It should become the definitive account of the intense controversies over plans for development of industries in Easter Ross.

It also has wider implications for other rural areas distant from cities. Lessons can be learned about the roles of public bodies and private investment, especially where conflicts of interest may occur.

For my own part, I remember well the occasion when

5

Willie Ross, Secretary of State for Scotland, (whom I succeeded in 1970) had to make his very significant statement, described in this book, announcing a resignation from the Highland Board, in response to a Question which I had tabled in the Commons for answer that day.

I am glad that the book starts with the threat to the railway lines from Inverness west to Kyle of Lochalsh and north to Wick. When I took office in 1970 these lines were about to be closed, but I persuaded my Cabinet colleagues that this should be stopped. Trains are still running on both lines 30 years later.

GORDON CAMPBELL

Introduction

T HIS IS the story of a row which put at risk the job of Willie Ross, then Secretary of State for Scotland, thirty years ago. It is a cautionary tale which still has lessons for today's newly established Scottish Parliament as it endeavours to increase employment opportunities. It shows what can happen to Government if control on unelected members of quangos is so lacking that it may be unaware of commitments made on its behalf. It makes clear the difficulty of being able to take advantage of the entrepreneurial abilities of successful businessmen without careful watch being kept on possible conflict between their public service and private profit.

This was the problem facing the author: what should you do if you discover that the quasi-Government body for whom you work is paying the substantial research and development costs for a possible foreign owned multi-million dollar petro-chemical complex promoted by the private company of one of its members, which could profit hugely should it proceed but need not repay any of these costs should it not?

What if you see Government being unwittingly committed to meeting the whole cost of the infrastructure for the development, including providing new port facilities, housing, schools, etc.? Staff of the newly established Highlands and Islands Development Board appeared unconcerned at how it was committing the unwitting

Government who set it up and appointed its members. The train of events appeared to be accelerating out of control, lacking any Government driver on the footplate.

After discussing my anxieties with Dr Ian Grimble, the Highland historian, early in 1967 I drew up and sent, privately through a Labour M.P., a memorandum to the Secretary of State detailing the facts which led to my anxieties and, lacking any assurance of action, followed it with a fortnight's ultimatum that, unless action was taken, I would "publish and be damned".

The text of this memorandum is published as an Appendix (page 125 *et seq.*) to this book, which records the history of the press and political row which followed. What I had not foreseen was that *The Times,* to whom I passed my information, would reveal its source and invite John Robertson, another HIDB member, to their office to help the writing of a laudatory article about the Board's plan.

This is also the story of the rise and fall of a charismatic and plausible adventurer, Frank Thomson, who very nearly succeeded in pulling off a remarkable self-enriching coup which could have changed the history of Easter Ross in the Scottish Highlands and its inhabitants. The proposal to site a polluting heavy industry beside a town in an agricultural area divided the community and even, sometimes, members of the same family. The farming community were accused of selfishly opposing an incoming industry which could help reduce local unemployment.

Press and politicians joined in during the three weeks it took till Frank Thomson's forced resignation, soon followed by that of John Robertson and the withdrawal of Occidental Oil.

PHIL DURHAM

Contents

Chapter One
Railway closures in Scotland

FOLLOWING the appointment by the Conservative Government in 1962 of an accountant/economist, Dr. Richard Beeching, to consider the reshaping of British Railways, the National Council on Inland Transport, a body chaired by a Labour peer Lord Stonham, in September sent a memorandum to Harold Macmillan, the Prime Minister. This suggested that the closure of all railway services and lines which, on the basis of comparing present earnings using the present method of railway costing, were found unprofitable, would be economically disastrous and socially intolerable. It sought a plan to be drawn up by Government to co-ordinate all freight and passenger services by rail, road, sea and air. From the reply on 7th February, 1963 of Ernest Marples, Minister of Transport it became even more clear that the main argument hinged on a comparison of the relative costs between providing rail track against that of maintaining roads, a comparison about as difficult as that between the relative returns of using hill land for forestry compared with hill farming.

A month later, on 27th March, the British Railways Board published "The Reshaping of British Railways" known thereafter as the Beeching Report. This proposed the withdrawal of passenger services on no fewer than 50 lines in Scotland, of which 42 would involve passenger and often line closures, while eight planned

11

cessation of local stopping trains on lines left open. No fewer than 470 Scottish stations would close.

Of immediate concern to those living north and west of Inverness was the proposed total abandonment of passenger services on the Inverness-Wick/Thurso and Inverness-Kyle lines, together with the future abandonment of stock wagons and reduction of fish and general freight services to wagon loads only. Two years earlier two distinguished Scottish law lords had produced the Cameron/Kilbrandon Report on transport services in the Highlands and Islands. This had stated that *"the value of peripheral services such as the Highland lines cannot of course be assessed properly by taking them on their own, apart from the main network. An operating loss on the fringes, taken by themselves, may be offset to some extent by the value of traffic which they bring to the rest of the undertaking, and the resulting net loss, in financial terms, may be acceptable to the undertaking as a whole as the cost of producing a comprehensive network of services"*. This concept of arteries and veins in the limbs feeding blood in and out of the trunk to maintain healthy circulation in the whole body had either been disregarded or not considered in the Beeching calculation.

Under the Railways Act, 1962 the future of railway services north and west of Inverness, and indeed of all other services threatened with closure, would be decided by Government, advised by the Transport Users' Consultative Committee (TUCC) who would report to the Minister of Transport after hearing evidence on any hardship involved in a closure, making any appropriate proposals for its alleviation. Should the cost of alternative services be too great, the Minister had the power to order the Railways Board to keep open a passenger service, with Government contributing to its cost.

During the summer of 1963 both national and local press was bombarded by angry letters of protest at pending Scottish rail closure proposals, not only from the Highlands but also from the Borders, the Ayrshire Coast, Fife, Angus and along the south coast of the Moray Firth. In the Highlands the fiery cross was hoisted high. The population north of the Great Glen temporarily abandoned such long-standing rivalries as Jacobite against Hanoverian, Presbyterian against Catholic, Laird against Crofter/ Tenant, sheep against trees, or Stalker/Ghillie against Poacher to present a united front against a proposed rail-less wilderness planned from the south. Industries from the size of Dounreay Atomic Station or Invergordon Distillery down to local garages, potato growers, stockmen, sea fishermen, salmon netsmen and coal merchants all united in a howl of protest.

It was only after a notice appeared in the press, that on 9th and 10th March 1964 in the Town House, Inverness the Scottish TUCC would hold its meeting to hear objections to the proposed abandonment of passenger services north and west of Inverness, that any concerted attempt to co-ordinate action to oppose such closures began. An informal meeting held in the Royal Hotel, Invergordon, since burnt down, agreed to form an association to that end. Most of those attending that initial meeting were farmers in Easter Ross. Eventually, after alternative suggestions had been considered and rejected, it was decided to name the organisation the North of Scotland Vigilantes Association. Prominent at that meeting were two men: Mr William Munro, proprietor of the Royal Garage, main Rootes Group dealer for the North of Scotland and friend of Sir William Rootes, and Mr Frank Thomson, a charismatic bearded figure who had been active in developing at Invergordon the largest grain distillery in Europe. Afterwards Mr Thomson invited everyone to meet in the Invergordon Distillers office ten days later, by which time a draft constitution could be agreed. That meeting appointed Thomson chairman, Munro vice-chairman and an incomer to the area, Fitzherbert Wright, an old Etonian, who travelled round in a vintage Rolls Royce and claimed, quite erroneously as it proved, to be on friendly terms with many of the old Etonians in the Government, secretary.

Mr Charles Jauncey, QC, was asked to act for the Association and public meetings were to be held in local halls spread over Caithness, Sutherland, Ross-shire and Inverness-shire. Information was sought on the likely effects rail closure would have on local businesses and individuals. Following favourable local press comment on the objectives of the Vigilantes, a further half dozen farmers joined the committee which decided to write and seek a meeting with Sir Alec Douglas Home who had replaced Macmillan as Prime Minister. Thirty individuals each agreed to subscribe £10 as start-up funding, with William Munro, Lord Lovat and auctioneer and farmer Peter McCallum as trustees. The local press agreed to print free of charge a Vigilante request that those concerned by the loss of their railway supply names, addresses and a five-shilling membership subscription.

By Christmas the temporary office set up was so inundated with letters that volunteer members had to help cope with the frenzy of interest. There was an offer of co-operation from the local-government supported North of Scotland Transport Conference, whose constitution prevented it taking the urgent action that the threat to Highland life required. A local artist had designed a kilted Thomas the Tank Engine type face named MacPuff which, not without some reservation, was accepted as a logo for the Vigilantes.

By the end of December, after the Prime Minister had agreed to receive a deputation from the Highlands in January, Easter Ross's most distinguished novelist and historian Eric Linklater, a Vigilante member, agreed to write the memorandum to be presented at 10 Downing Street. Already public meetings had been held both in Aberdeen and Perth, where other feeder railway lines were under threat of closure. The proposal of John Rollo, chairman of the Highland Fund and later to become vice-chairman of the Highlands and Islands Development Board, to drop North of Scotland and become the Scottish Vigilantes Association and to widen the remit to supporting opposition to rail closures throughout Scotland was accepted. Events were moving fast, support was flooding in and it rapidly became apparent that Fitzherbert Wright was not coping, with the temporary office in chaos. After I had agreed to address a planned NFU rally to be held in an Inverness auction mart on rail closures, I agreed to take over from him as Vigilante secretary.

Since war time sea service and two years of submarine command, I had courted and married an Easter Ross farmer's daughter, only six weeks later in Londonderry to collapse with polio, ending up in a wheel chair for life. As well as farming the hill farm of Scotsburn where we lived and helping my father in law with his farm accounts and the wage payments of twenty employees, I had built up and run a co-operative egg and poultry packing station but was happy to turn over its day to day running and accept the new challenge as secretary of both the Scottish Vigilantes and the Transport Conference of Scotland, with a remit to prevent and delay railway closures under the Transport Act 1962 and help industry with similar objectives, which it had spawned.

At the meeting in 10 Downing Street on 27th January, 1964 Colin Campbell, a Sutherland sheep farmer, and Frank Thomson presented Eric Linklater's memorandum and represented the North. Also present were Lord Polwarth, chair of the Scottish Council for Development and Industry and TUC Chairman, James Jack, both of whom spoke, and, for the Government, the Prime Minister, Ernest Marples, Minister of Transport, and Michael Noble, Secretary of State for Scotland. The PM emphasised that both the Scottish Council and the Transport Conference would have access to Mr Noble to oppose closures on social and economic grounds. Three of us attended the Elgin TUCC hearing to observe procedure. This dealt with the planned closure of lines to Lossiemouth and along the South coast of the Moray Firth to Banff, and allowed me to draft an advice letter for distribution to objectors who approached us, making clear that what was needed was a personal statement of the likely effect on their lives of the abandonment of passenger rail services, with particular reference to any hardship the proposed road alternative would cause them.

We encouraged objectors to attend the TUCC hearing but offered to represent those unable or unwilling to attend, agreeing, after collecting evidence from the points each made, to forward on their individual letters. Once more the local press printed our advice letter free and, in leaders, commended our efforts.

Working long hours for shortage of time and abstracting the more striking hardship cases from the 165 letters, which we numbered before forwarding on to the TUCC, we produced twenty minutes of evidence to be given by three separate speakers. The first was headed "The case against rail closures according to Cameron/Kilbrandon". Its first two paragraphs read:-

"We wish, in opening our case, to call attention to the statement made by the Chairman of the TUCC for Scotland that he did not think the attitude of the Scottish Vigilantes Association, who had organised some of the objectors, was very helpful. May we say we are here to be helpful to the TUCC, to the 165 objectors we are directly representing, and to many others whom we have helped with their objections, but who objected individually.

With your permission, Sir, we propose to take our facts from a Ministry of Transport White Paper published in 1963 and headed "Transport Services in the Highlands and Islands". We believe that the Committee are to report to the Minister of Transport and we are hopeful that he will be prepared to accept facts from his own White Paper and even, perhaps, find them helpful in considering the two passenger services under threat of closure today."

It then proceeded to summarise this report by two distinguished Scottish Law Lords and recalled that Lord Cameron, the Chairman of the Government's advisory Highland Panel, had stated at their recent meeting:-

"There is very good reason to think that the Railway Board's figures do not present a whole or accurate picture of the accounting position in relation to passenger services, and that it may well be that fuller disclosure of figures would produce a very

16

different picture of the real costs and real deficiencies – if any – to provide services even on their present scale. He had continued that he and all members of the advisory Highland Panel wished to state publicly that, if the threatened closures were to take place, they would all resign as there would be no purpose in their continuing to advise Mr Noble, the Secretary of State for Scotland."

Following on from this opening, two further articulate speakers would deal with likely hardship on Inverness-Wick/Thurso and Inverness-Kyle routes, respectively.

At 10.30 on the morning of 9th March, the hearing opened in the impressive council chambers of the Town House, Inverness. On a raised platform sat the TUCC members with, below, the Railway Board representatives facing about fifty objectors, with press and television on the cross benches. Following the Chairman's introduction, British Rail began its evidence in support of Dr Beeching's proposed closures. It appeared a sterile procedure where objectors were precluded from contesting the statistical statements they trotted out. When the sitting adjourned for lunch, the chamber was cleared but, being up two flights of stairs from the pavement below, I was allowed to remain inside in my wheel chair; a mistake: the temptation was too great. Here was I alone in an empty room with the railway briefing papers lying open opposite me. From what I read it was clear they were well aware of the weakness of the argument that the alternative bus services were adequate.

In the afternoon, on completion of the railway evidence, with no opportunity of cross examination, it was the turn of the Vigilantes to give evidence on behalf of the 165 objectors we represented. Following the Cameron-Kilbrandon summary, direct evidence pinpointing the hardship likely to be suffered by those using the Inverness-Wick/Thurso line were it to be closed was given by a new speaker referring also to evidence from Dounreay Nuclear Station, Caithness Glass, T.M.Hunter Wool Mills, Brora and Patersons salmon netsmen, amongst many others, of the importance of passenger trains in moving urgent perishable and bulky supplies which could not be transported by bus. Perhaps the most striking letter came from Dr Duncan Fraser, Moderator-elect of the General Assembly of the Church of Scotland, who contended that the work of the Kirk in the North and West would be affected, in some cases very seriously. The quite different routes followed by road and rail received a mention.

Finally our last witness dealt with the proposed Kyle line closure, emphasising the completely unrealistic bus service timetable from Kyle to Dingwall offered as a railway replacement. She quoted a 1963 White Paper stating that both A832 and A890 to be used by Highland Omnibuses were single carriageway with passing places, of poor alignment and already 50% overloaded; road traffic was required to cross Loch Carron on the privately-owned Strome Ferry which was not licensed to run in darkness, was limited to carrying only sixty passengers on each crossing and was subject to interruption in stormy weather. There was no shelter on the ferries and bus passengers were required to vacate their seats and thus old and young, sick or healthy alike, might be soaked in bad weather, needing to continue their bus journey in this condition. In a recent statement to the Traffic Commissioners the operating company had stated they had allowed nine minutes for passengers joining and alighting, one minute for each of the nine stops, and eight minutes for the ferry crossing with a further three minutes for delays, making 20 minutes stopping time in all, which gave them 2 hours 55 minutes to move 87 1/2 miles, an average speed of 30 mph. Those living in the area knew that the nine foot wide road from Auchentyre to Garve could not be traversed by an ordinary car at a safer average speed than 20 mph. They also knew of the possible two-hour delays at the ferry in summer time, and of road dangers in wintry conditions.

During the 1962/63 winter drifts closed the road, but the rail service continued. She next mentioned two Dingwall teachers commuting daily from their homes in Lochluichart by train, unable to get to work in time in the proposed alternative bus. Her final summing up was that inhabitants in the West resented the offer of such utterly unrealistic alternative services and claimed that this appeared to them a deliberate plot to deceive and mislead the TUCC. As his Ministry owned Highland Omnibuses, it appeared the Minister of Transport, to whom the TUCC would report, must accept responsibility for suggesting this misleading alternative. After all individuals had been given their chance to speak, the second day of the Inverness hearing concluded, leaving the TUCC members to consider their report to Mr Marples.

The Scottish TUCC held further hardship hearings in Forfar, Grantown on Spey, the Borders and Glasgow, all attended by the Vigilantes. At a meeting of the Transport Conference in Perth, John Rollo, representing the Scottish Council (Development & Industry) agreed to produce a report for them on the likely effects on business of Beeching closures. Then a large contingent from the North led by Eric Linklater, with enthusiastic support from Gaeldom, held a rally opposing rail closures in the Highlanders' Institute, Glasgow. The publicity generated persuaded the Railway Board to agree to meet representatives of the Scottish Council, N.F.U., Highland Panel and Transport Conference (into which local government had merged the North of Scotland Conference). At this meeting British Rail agreed, once the Inverness lines had been spared, to set up a Highland liaison body with users.

Already Thomson's suggestion of the Vigilantes commissioning a study of Highland Opportunity to make more use of the railway, the subject of the next chapter, had been agreed and Professor E.R. Hondelink, Transport Consultant and Economist to the United Nations and World Bank, who had expressed concern at Dr Beeching's Plan, had offered to produce for the Transport Conference an alternative Scottish Transport Plan to co-ordinate road, rail, sea and air freight and passenger services.

The Highland Railway Users' Council with an informative, consultative and advisory role, held its inaugural meeting in

Inverness in September, two months after Highland lines had been reprieved. Attended by interested users, it agreed to meet two-monthly, chaired alternately by the newly appointed Manager, Highland Lines and the County Clerk of Ross & Cromarty.

Rail operation was undergoing great change. Already 2,500 diesel locomotives were working, with the remaining 4,500 steam engines due to be replaced and scrapped by 1967. Signalling had been modernised and, despite the doubts of HRUC users, management decided to lift and scrap the second line over Drumochter Pass, 1,600 feet above sea level , only ten years later to have to replace it at considerable unnecessary cost when the single line with passing places proved inadequate. Turntables, no longer essential with reversible diesel traction, were scrapped, no one foreseeing the future demand for steam-headed tourist traffic twenty years later.

The Beeching proposed phasing out of stock and fish wagons would be likely to prove detrimental to the Highlands dependent on transporting the products of land and sea. Annually over 5,000 cattle and 20,000 sheep were moved from local stations to auction marts and south therefrom, quite apart from the 40,000 lambs sold on one August day each year at Lairg, Sutherland, generating several trainloads south from sidings there, the largest sheep sale in the world. The important Easter Ross and Black Isle seed potato trade involved careful straw insulation of rail wagons for frost protection before loading each with ten tons of bagged seed potatoes at local station sidings. Herring and white fish landings at Mallaig and Kyle of Lochalsh travelled speedily to Billingsgate in fish wagons, often hitched on the end of regular passenger trains.

Lacking dairy herds, the Western Isles were entirely dependent on the rail connection with MacBraynes ferry for the daily delivery of fresh milk and of all the everyday needs of daily life. Such matters occupied the two-monthly HRUC meetings which proved a useful way of discussing such vital traffic as well as passenger fares, inaccurate timetables, delays caused by on-request train stops at unmanned halts, advertising and the selling of services. One such meeting took place on rail, travelling from Inverness to Wick and back in the Manager's Inspection Saloon hitched to the rear of a regular passenger train. For the centenary in September 1965 of the opening of the Dava Moor direct link between Aviemore and Inverness, the historic yellow steam locomotive HR 103 and two contemporary passenger coaches were abstracted from the Glasgow Rail Museum to run several daily trips from Inverness to Forres, carrying full loads of tourists and rail buffs.

At the invitation of the *Financial Times* , as secretary of the Transport Conference of Scotland, I wrote a long article outlining the Hondelink idea for a co-ordinated policy for road, rail, sea and air services headed "Planning for Transport", which provoked some interesting correspondence but little else.

Then, following the modernisation of Inverness station with new booking hall, restaurant, loos and locked baggage storage lockers behind a new facade, the rail management abandoned the post of Manager, Highland Lines and Highlands and Islands Development Board took over HRUC's liaison work. The Vigilantes office closed, with the Scottish Railway Development Association taking over the work of the Transport Conference of Scotland, and so ended a chapter.

Chapter Two
Highland Opportunity.

W HEN BY the end of March 1964 it seemed safe to assume that the railway lines north and west of Inverness would be spared closure, Frank Thomson, chairing a Vigilante meeting, suggested that ways of generating traffic thereon ought now to be considered. His company Invergordon Distillers had worked with a firm of London consultants and he suggested the Vigilantes ought to commission them to consider and recommend ways of increasing economic development of Highland resources. He had discovered it would cost £1,500 to do this. A farm worker's annual wage at that time was £400 and this sort of expenditure was a completely new prospect to those whose interest was just to avert rail closures. Thomson persuasively waved their financial anxieties aside convincing them that raising covenanted subscriptions to meet such a trifling cost would be simple. His having promised to provide a seven-year covenant of £1,000 a year, the meeting, with one resignation, eventually agreed to commission the report, temporarily meeting its cost by voluntary interest free loans until such time as a prospectus for fund raising had been produced.

Chairing both the Scottish Vigilantes Association and the Transport Conference of Scotland, Frank Thomson, a chartered accountant incomer from Aberdeen, had earlier persuaded Max

Rayne of London Merchant Securities to put up the finance to take over the partly built grain distillery at Invergordon and complete it. With an annual capacity of ten million gallons of whisky, this became the largest grain distillery in Europe. Thomson had then formed a distillery pipe band which won the European Pipe Championship, taken over the ailing Ross County Football Club and then successfully tempted the mighty Glasgow Rangers team to travel north and play a friendly game on their Dingwall park, and was later to be elected Rector of Aberdeen University, no mean self publicity performance.

North arrived Michael Taylor, a transport economist with Martech Consultants, whose study on door to door rail transport carried out for British Rail was the basis for their new liner train development linking container handling depots by permanently-connected hydraulically-braked trains of flat wagons. As we collected information from county development officers and many others with an interest in an increased future Highland prosperity, Michael and I worked well with each other and formed a lasting friendship. Later he and his family would move north from the Midlands to settle on the West Coast and start a new bus service.

The Martech Report examined areas of opportunity in marketing the produce of land and sea, urging Highlanders to exploit their own resources, add value locally, especially to products of small size and high value, and try to create volume flows and export.

It was completed in two parts, the publication of the first of which was delayed till after the autumn general election which replaced Sir Alec Douglas Home's Tory Government with a Labour one under Harold Wilson. This delay allowed me time to design the cover of what the Vigilantes published as "Highland Opportunity". Drawing an outline map of the Highlands, swinging the mainland a few degrees anti-clockwise, exaggerating the sizes of Orkney and Shetland islands and moving them closer to the mainland, allowed me to produce a striking white land silhouette floating in a vivid red sea in which I was well pleased. Thirty years later many of its suggestions have born fruit, with hydroponics at Achiltibuie, a large board mill at Dalcross, Elphin marble exported to Italy by the train load through the Channel Tunnel, fish farming, tweed and textile development, bottling of water and much else.

One important section of the unpublished part two was to suggest possible uses of the large quantities of surplus carbon dioxide discharged by Invergordon Distillery. This resulted in it commissioning a far more expensive and detailed study of possible markets for by-products of this wasted CO_2 with Vigilante members being assured by Thomson that it was a safe assumption that the distillery would meet a considerable proportion of the cost of the Martech Report, once again alleviating their, as it later proved, justifiable anxieties over its financing. This second study, later to provoke arguments over its cost when it was made available to the future Highlands and Islands Development Board, was largely written for Proplan, a division of Martech Consultants, by Dr Jonathan Jenkins, a Cambridge natural sciences graduate who had worked as a senior research fellow at Sheffield University studying rocket combustion, supersonics, magneto hydrodynamics, fuel cells and high speed instrumentation. A sunken-eyed boffin, Jenkins also was later to become closely involved with the soon to be appointed Highlands and Islands Development Board and, in particular with one of its members, John Robertson, with whom he set up a chemical company, Hy-Chem. His study examined in detail the production of urea and other products which would require the availability of large quantities of cheap electricity. In addition to its fertiliser potential as a source of nitrogen, urea had wide uses in the plastics industry.

While Frank Thomson did deposit sufficient funds to maintain the rented office in Invergordon and the modest salaries of myself and my most intelligent and experienced American part-time secretary, there was no money to pay for the Martech report, all available funds being used to meet the cost of producing the

Hondelink plan for an integrated Scottish transport system, a draft of which had been passed to Eric Linklater to edit in November. Already I and the honorary treasurer were voicing anxieties about finance, an appeal for help from the local authority-funded North of Scotland Transport Conference having been turned down. Sir John Brooke, a laird who had joined the Trustees, resigned, unhappy at our ever widening activities beyond our original remit of saving the Highland railway lines.

Then, at a committee meeting in November 1964, Thomson in the Chair reported the formation by himself and Colin Campbell of the Polyscot group of companies which he emphasised were private and quite separate from any Vigilante activities which might follow from the publication of 'Highland Opportunity'. Polyscot Group, an association of existing companies, had formed a bank and an insurance company and their first development was to produce Polycast plastic in Campbell's home farm steading. Thomson invited any of the 17 members at the meeting to invest in Polyscot. He suggested its prospectus to the public would look for £3 million and he believed Lord Cameron in the chair of the Government's advisory Highland Panel had referred to this future project at its recent meeting. They looked for the participation of several large companies of 250 to 1,000 employees. While sounding most impressive, such large sums of money and expectations lay well beyond the experience of the ordinary farmers and businessmen serving on the Vigilante committee, such developers' kite flying, adding an extra nought or two for effect, being totally new to them. Everyone did know well and like Colin Campbell, who had inherited a deer forest/hill sheep farm in central Sutherland, as well as a low ground farm where his parents lived in a substantial house. His grandfather, as a result of Border farmers moving up to the Highlands with their Cheviot sheep after the evictions in the mid nineteenth century, had prospered to farm nearly 50,000 acres of deer forest at Corriemuilzie and Forest Farm, an empty area of mid Ross-Shire and Sutherland with a lodge, deer stalking, salmon fishing, numerous hill trout lochs and wild isolation. Colin had worked for the Westminster Estates as managing director of Sutherland Transport and Trading Company, serving all the vast area north and west of the railhead at Lairg, running its garage, buses, mail contract, lorries, coal business and much else. He piloted his own plane from an airstrip at Balblair Farm and entertained friends and their children to magical weeks in the ramshackle Corriemuilzie Lodge, whose main door entered through the bathroom, while the sitting room window looked west to the majestic peaks of Sguirr and Beneach.

Concern about the future development and proper use of the land resource of the region was shared by other organisations. For some years I had been an active member of SPALDA, the Scottish Peat and Land Development Association and, at this time, they held a meeting and press conference in Edinburgh University on the world food situation, with particular emphasis on future development of the hill lands of Scotland, which generated wide publicity.

Of the 2,000 copies of 'Highland Opportunity' we printed, all but 450 sold in the first two months but this only achieved a small reduction in the Vigilantes' overdraft. Again Thomson suggested funding would be forthcoming from either Invergordon Distillers or possibly from Invergordon Chemical Enterprises, a company newly set up to promote a petro-chemical complex in Invergordon. Meantime it was hoped that Angus, where we had helped with their TUCC hearing, would contribute to the costs of the Transport Conference whose overdraft Thomson had promised to guarantee.

When the *Guardian* wrote to enquire when the prospectus promised for the development company at our earlier Highlanders Institute meeting would be available, Thomson told me to reply he was working on a draft but needed more time. I was visited by the *Times* Scottish Correspondent who wrote a long article, supported by a leader, on the resurgence of economic hope in the Highlands. Meanwhile the Vigilante office was kept busy in correspondence with many supporters of our efforts and ideas, amongst them distinguished inhabitants like Drs Fraser Darling, Lorne Campbell from the Isle of Canna and Ian Grimble.

When in March 1965 the Vigilantes held their first annual general meeting, our Chairman at the last moment sent his regrets, due to Invergordon Distillers being about to float in a few days as a public company. At the committee meeting preceding the AGM it was agreed that, in his absence, it would be pointless to discuss finance, loans and future funding. Eric Linklater was persuaded to chair the AGM, which accepted that the Labour Government's proposed formation of a Highland Development Board should in no way be allowed to delay the developments signposted by Martech Consultants. The well-attended meeting offered its support to our continuing transport and economic activities. Without any specific activity or firm financial proposals, such support was meaningless and a further six months elapsed before Thomson managed to find the time to attend a meeting.

To complete this account of the production of 'Highland Opportunity' and its results, the following extracts from the minutes of two meetings of the Scottish Vigilantes Association demonstrate how, in the hope of its Chairman's dream becoming reality, its members continued to exist in a cloud of euphoria.

"**28th September, 1965.** Mr Thomson said that, four years ago, he began searching for an outlet for the by-products of Invergordon Distillery and, two years ago, the Vigilantes revealed that there were people who were individually keen to do something to improve the state of the Highlands, none of whom had co-operated with others with the same aim.

"The Martech report was authorised and out of the Vigilantes' contact with Martech came useful investigations for Invergordon Distillery. They got in touch with the Product Planning branch of Martech, in particular with Jonathan Jenkins, and those studies revealed two revolutionary chemical processes. When he set out to grasp this unique chemical opportunity, many attempts were made to site the plant elsewhere, particularly in Newfoundland. Very influential oil and chemical interests tried to oppose it, but this complex is going to be built at Invergordon. It is already fully backed with real money, the sales contracts have been made, but the thing lacking is the necessary infrastructure. Roads, houses, rail connections and the port had to be designed. The complex would employ directly 2,700 which meant that, with their families, 11 or 12 thousand people would be needed within ten years.

"The main snag did not lie in the finance for the complex; it lay in the planning required, which would have an enormous impact on Invergordon Town Council, Ross-shire County Council, the Secretary of State and the future Highland Development Board. There would be about 150 people earning £5,000 a year to house, and 20 to 30 of these would earn over £10,000. The complex would be run by a man of Dr Beeching's standing earning £25,000 a year and already two men of this calibre are prepared to come. There will also be an influx of Americans. Advance notice of the development was leaked out by those opposing it but it has already been lobbied and accepted by both the Government and Opposition.

"The development will not just affect Invergordon, in fact Invergordon will become a large blot on the landscape. The people will need to be housed elsewhere, either in Alness, Evanton and Dingwall, or in Tain, or probably in a completely new town. The studies for the scheme will be complete in six months. The oil refinery and cement works could be complete in eighteen months, but a third of the total employees would by then be needed and it appeared impossible to house them. The whole scheme was likely to cost in excess of £35 million and, in addition, £20 million of the profits would be ploughed back to make an investment of £60 million in six years. The whole complex would be British controlled and arrangements had been made that equity shares in it would be made available locally and that sufficient of the fertiliser production to meet local demand and for land reclamation would also be locally available.

Mr Thomson emphasised that he had no need to start this tremendous operation but he believed that it would solve the Highland problem once and for all, not in small pieces but in one operation. It would bring technical schools and work for the children in the Region, particularly for the abler children. It would inevitably involve inconvenience to many and would be very hard on some farms where land had been farmed by the same family for generations.

"**7th October, 1965.** Mr Durham suggested that we must hold a meeting of the Transport Conference just to offer its management to someone else and made the point that, had we been repaid the £2,000 debt of the Transport Conference, and had Invergordon Distillers made the contribution promised on 7th September 1964, we should be able to meet all our debts. Members had expressed disquiet at the financial situation at every meeting held over the past year and the time had come to deal with it before discussing anything else.

"Mr Thomson said it was only reasonable to suppose that finance would be forthcoming from either Invergordon Distillers or Invergordon Chemicals to clear our debts. Mr Butler, the honorary treasurer, said he agreed that, now we know our finance is covered, we can happily discuss the future.

"Later in the meeting to decide the future of the Vigilantes and Transport Conference Thomson suggested that those who had made loans should write them off and that Martech should write off the cost of their report in view of the profit they would make on work for the new complex. To this statement Mr Taylor replied that a separate firm were working on the complex and he had a number of facts relevant to this but he would not embarrass Mr Thomson by discussing them in public.

"Mr Durham pointed out that, even were all these debts to be written off, £800 would be needed to close the office and repay the overdraft. At that Mr Thomson said he would sign a guarantee form."

Thus, without any agreement on debt cancellation, the association drew to an inconclusive close. Just eighteen months would elapse to disprove the bold statement that finance was no problem and prove that many of Thomson's statements would stretch even the vivid imagination of Walter Mitty.

Chapter Three
Highlands and Islands Development Board

W ITH THE closure of the Vigilante office in Invergordon
I was left with a need for extra income to add to that
from the farm and my Naval disability pension. Thus it
was most welcome that, during the first month of the establishment
of the new Highlands and Islands Development Board, I was
invited to call at their office and told my knowledge of Highland
transport, land use and social problems would be of value to them
and offered a three day a week part time job as project officer,
which sounded rather grand, at a modest salary of £50 a month,
which did not. With my interest in the Highland future and despite
a 40 mile journey to and from Inverness, with the A9 winding
round the ends of both Cromarty and Beauly firths – no firth
bridges then – I accepted the job.

I have often felt that Britain's rulers in Westminster, and
perhaps closer in St Andrews House, Edinburgh, seek to administer
half the area of Scotland by a form of distant colonial rule. They
knew what was best for the natives and, with a firm hand, offered
the necessary support and subsidy to keep them from active revolt.
When the Labour Government passed an Act on 5th August 1965
setting up a Board "which shall have a general function of
preparing, concerting, promotion, assisting and undertaking
measures for the economic and social development of the

Highlands" there seemed better hope for the future. To advise this new body would be appointed a Consultative Council, most of whose members had earlier served on the Highland Panel under the chairmanship of Lord Cameron, DSC, QC, who would continue in the chair of the new body.

Appointed to chair the new Board was a civil servant, ex Chief Planner in St Andrews House who, despite lacking academic background, had become Professor of Planning in Glasgow University. I later came to find Professor Robert Grieve pompous, vain and humourless, his only scope to use his urban planning experience being the fertile red sandstone belt down the east coast from Orkney to Easter Ross and the Black Isle, the geology of the vast infertile area north and west and in the islands supporting only sparse population. It was an odd and unimaginative choice. His ambition to plan an urban "string of pearls" to accommodate a population of quarter of a million souls round the periphery of the Cromarty and Beauly firths was unrealistic. It began to founder from his failure to recognise that, in promoting the seminal industrial development, the use of Board funds with considerable financial benefit to one of his fellow members might be considered unethical and he proved utterly incapable of taking the ruthless action needed to avoid a public scandal. The unfavourable publicity dented the credibility of the Board on which so many in the Higlands had built such hopes.

The Vice Chairman of HIDB, who has already featured in this account, was very different. John Rollo was a practical engineer who, as chairman of the Highland Fund, a voluntary organisation supported by industrial donations and some local government finance, had for many years offered small-scale financial and managerial assistance to small rural businesses in the region. He thus well understood the traditions of the area and its inhabitants, though his concern for indigenous rather than outside endeavour did not always find favour with his fellow Board members.

He was dragged unwillingly behind the ambitions of the majority of his fellow members to promote heavy industry in the region.

As soon as the Government's intention to set up HIDB was announced, lobbying over who should sit on it began. Apart from a trade union member and an industrialist to be appointed, it was clear there would need to be one member to represent farming, forestry and stock rearing which, with their peripheral suppliers, formed the main economic activity of the Highlands.

Serving on the Highland Panel had been two leading farm contenders. Both had been active in the National Farmers Union. One was John C Robertson, with a double first at university and a military OBE for his service as a pilot in the RAF volunteer reserve, who was young and ambitious, the son of a prominent farmer with extensive interests both in Easter Ross and as a west coast sheep farmer. Obstinate to the point of rudeness should anyone of long practical experience doubt the practicality of his analytically calculated solution to some problem or other, John was often just too cerebral. He was to become one of the two Board members to be most involved in the promotion of plans to introduce major heavy industry to the region.

The other farming contender was Reay D G Clarke who farmed on a smaller scale, was older and more traditional in his belief that more profitable land use would be achieved by protection of the scarce workable arable low ground land and the better development of integrated afforestation and improvement of the plentiful poorer marginal hill land. This view was supported by the three colleges of agriculture.

Amongst those consulted on this choice was Alasdair Mackenzie, the newly elected Liberal MP for Ross and Cromarty and himself a practical Gaelic speaking farmer. He told me he favoured Clarke but was persuaded to recommend Robertson and, in the end, Robertson won the appointment.

The fourth full-time member appointed was Prophet Smith

with a fishing industry and trade union background and a long-time record of Labour support. In addition to the four full-time members were two part-time: Willie Logan, a local man who had built up a large building and construction firm from small beginnings during the Second World War and had been involved with Freeson's endeavours to establish a local air service using short take-off and landing Islander aircraft on primitive grass runways to serve small island communities in Orkney, Shetland and the north mainland. This service became Loganair, eventually to be swallowed by British Airways. The other was William Scholes, with an education, training and availability of skilled labour remit.

Five civil servants from the Department of Agriculture and Fisheries for Scotland were seconded to staff the new board. The Secretary, having previously been secretary to the Highland Panel, had the advantage of knowing what advice they had previously given Government. Bobby Fasken was a decent honest and straightforward man later to be out of his depth in trying to deal with a major industrial development plan, posing a possible conflict of interest between Government and those promoting it, and rapidly getting out of hand.

His assistant had been sent packing from a post advising President Nyere in Tanganyika. The appointment of this man, still affecting an EAS nationality number plate, seemed evidence of happiness to transfer a plodder from one colony to their Highland colony: at least it moved him out from under their feet.

To serve the Consultative Council was Tom Johnston, who seemed to find it difficult to show proper respect to many of its experienced members.

When on 1st December 1965 I first reported for work in the rented office in a modern block behind Inverness Library I was given a desk in a spacious room containing a dozen plastic tables and chairs and little else, with only one other occupant. John Robertson came down from his office on the floor above to talk about HIDB's possible future activities and tell me that it would be helpful to Board members and senior staff to have a resumé from the local, technical and national Press of items which might appear to be of relevance and they would like me to produce it. Thus I began to produce my twice weekly "From the papers". This allowed me a unique opportunity to summarise items that I felt ought to be of concern to them, whether they were or not.

Everything in HIDB's office in those early days was informal and unstructured, with Board members and staff often dropping in for a chat. Thus I renewed my acquaintance with John Rollo and met Grieve and Prophet Smith. No one seemed to have any clear idea of what to do or how to do it. Then, at the first Highland Board Christmas party with only about twenty people there, Grieve gave a welcoming speech ending by suggesting he thought it would be helpful were any of those present to express their ideas how best the Board should meet its remit.

John Rollo's view that it ought to concentrate on encouraging Highlanders to engage in locally based industry, the support of which often involved making available quite modest sums that they were unable to borrow elsewhere, seemed admirable. He said they needed grants, loans and managerial advice and we should beware of inexperienced outsiders seeking to make a fast buck by taking advantage of more generous finance than was available elsewhere, Improved transport and communications were needed to assist the development of indigenous industry. All this echoed the "Highland Opportunity" ideas.

John Robertson believed the Board should be ruthless in its attempts to find and encourage large scale industries using the most modern technology. He instanced Dounreay, Fort William paper mill and Invergordon Distillery as the type of industries to foster and encourage. Only such major developments combined with tourism would be sufficient to halt the population decline in the region. He doubted if we'd ever solve our problems without developing such growth.

Prophet Smith felt there was scope to develop the pelagic,

demersal and shell fisheries by assistance both to boat building and equipment and the improvement of fish landing and handling facilities. He sought early recruitment of a specialist employee with wide knowledge and experience of the fishing industry.

Perhaps unwisely I ventured a hope that HIDB would tackle land use and ownership, especially concentrating on the peripheral north and west mainland and islands. With hindsight it was unwise for a very new and junior employee to have the temerity to express his ideas. The civil servants kept quiet. Later, when I was called to a Board meeting to speak to a paper I had written, Grieve was heard to comment he wished that fellow Durham would not constantly try to tell Board members what to do.

Suitably fortified everyone went home for Christmas resolved really to get down to work in the New Year.

Entered in the minutes of the second HIDB Plenary meeting was:

"Mr P Durham, who has a broad knowledge of Highland affairs, has been engaged to make a digest of press reports at a fee of £50 a month."

I continued to produce "From the papers" till I was relieved of the task when the secretary of the Consultative Council, Tom Johnson, started to circulate actual press cuttings extracted with scissors and photocopied. By then Robertson had set me a project, which took till November to complete, of studying export markets for seed potatoes, one of Easter Ross and Black Isle's more important crops because their latitude and cool climate reduced virus and disease problems compared with the South.

John himself grew this crop at Castlecraig, marketed by John O Gordon, the largest seed potato merchant in the area, who rented a large shed originally used during the war for mine-filling from John for one of his potato businesses. My research, involving consultation with trade attachés in a dozen potato growing areas, identified the varieties and tonnage grown in each country, many of which varieties lacked a British market. The main demand was for

'Up to date' and 'Arran Banner'. I received much help from the Department of Agriculture and the Agricultural Colleges. Each country proved to have different health regulations. Apart from South Africa, most potato growing took place in countries round the Mediterranean where the potato disease 'blackleg' appeared the major problem. In the summer Dr Marais and a colleague from the South African trade division met John and me and later John O Gordon and two other seed potato merchants. Their requirement for washed potatoes limited the outlet to Gordon with the only potato washing plant in the building owned by Robertson. My research paper was made widely available to the potato trade but sadly a major Highland export potato trade failed to develop.

Another project was to examine whether a useful tourist encouragement might develop from the introduction of sand yachting on suitable beaches. Some of the longest stretches of sand in Britain lay on the west of the Outer Hebrides so, armed with Dr Chris Smout's geographic studies of the Uists and Benbecula, I took the ferry there to be captivated by the long isolated stretches of shell sand outside the wild flower strewn machair of South Uist, where the sounds of Atlantic breakers were punctuated by calls of pewit, oystercatcher and occasional corncrake. It seemed to me a shame to disturb by human activity this fifteen mile unbroken stretch of empty beach and, fortunately, lack of available accommodation did prevent any such development there.

With the encouragement of the Caithness County Development Officer, a meeting was held in the Northern Sands Hotel, Dunnett. As well as the chairman and secretary of the British Federation of Sand and Land Yacht Clubs, who came with a pair of sand yachts towed behind their car, it was attended by about twenty five interested individuals who watched them tack and reach on Dunnett sands, and after dinner in the adjoining hotel, formed the Caithness Sand and Land Yacht Club, purchasing the two sand yachts before the party broke up in the small hours.

These projects were overshadowed by my involvement in

making a study of possible development and expansion of youth activities in the region. From outside the area, two imaginative initiatives in using its environment came to my notice. One, for which HIDB's financial support was sought, was the Inverlair Lodge field centre run by a committee chaired by Lord Kilbrandon and organised by Mr R.F. Mackenzie, the unconventional headmaster of Braehead Junior Secondary School in Fife, whose book, *Escape from the Classroom,* had awakened wide interest.

They had obtained the use of Inverlair Lodge in Strath Roy and planned to renovate it as a field centre for their pupils from a depressed mining area threatened by pit closure using volunteer labour. Lord Kilbrandon, a distinguished law lord, had written suggesting the Board should contribute £10 towards the cost of a week's essential work there involving Borstal boys and other volunteers. After phoning Mr Mackenzie who agreed this sum was ridiculously inadequate and, facing possible contempt, I altered the sum in his handwritten letter to £200 and, my wickedness undetected, this sum was voted as a social grant. I travelled there to find over twenty workers re-pointing walls, repairing doors, floors and panelling, scraping off old wallpaper and generally starting to make good twenty years' dilapidation. The grant had helped with the cost of transport and food, while the Forestry Commission had been generous with the supply of wood and the loan of equipment. Led by two teachers and a warder in charge of the Borstal boys, everyone seemed to be working with a will. The Countess of Mar and Kellie, in the chair of Enterprise Youth Scotland, was also there lending a hand.

The other outside development was initiated by a trust established by an inner London school at the bottom end of Loch Awe in Argyll. They were developing the site of the Royal Engineer-demolished Inverliever Lodge and, having raised the considerable sum of £20,000, were building a kitchen to feed 90, with accompanying dining hall/assembly room and a dormitory for 20, allowing for another 20 under canvas. It was hoped that 500 boys and girls a year would spend a week being introduced to such activities as sailing, canoeing, climbing, wild life study and other open air activities. This well-funded trust was able to pay some skilled labour and, aided by volunteers, the work was progressing well when I visited the site.

Sadly I was unable to discover any similar initiatives to allow Highland children, many in term time away from home in hostels, such opportunities to learn about such activities in their home environment.

After five months' research and having consulted over 100 organisations and individuals, including Alec Dickson, who had started and still controlled Community Service Volunteers, and educationalists like Professors O'Dell and George Houston, I produced an eighteen foolscap page report, with a further eighteen pages of appendices, summarising the evidence I had collected. My principal finding was that youth activities could not be considered separately from education, of which they were or should be a part. I recommended that HIDB should without delay commission a research study into Highland and Island education and that of Scandinavian countries who face similar problems. When this recommendation was considered by the Board, they passed it on to the Consultative Council who, after I had spoken about it at their June meeting, passed it on to their newly appointed education sub-committee who invited me to join them.

Thus I found myself meeting James Shaw Grant, Chairman of the Crofters Commission, Naomi Mitchison, Kay Matheson, one of the four who had abstracted the Stone of Destiny from Westminster Abbey, Farquhar Mackintosh from Skye, Charles Macleod, an Inverness School Inspector who had recently visited Norway, and Edward Thomason, Chairman of Shetland Education Committee.

This Education Sub-committee met two-monthly in the Board office and I found their discussions informed, wide-ranging, full of practical common sense and enjoyable. In November they were

addressed by R F Mackenzie on his ideas and hopes both for
Inverlair and for others to follow where they had led, and by C
Macleod on Norwegian educational practice in maintaining
excellence in the peripheral communities in the north mainland and
islands where every effort was made to return children home from
school at weekends. They recommended that the Board should
continue to offer support for Inverlair.

The following two meetings I attended were almost entirely
devoted to trying to answer the questions I had posed in my report,
the second held on 24th February 1967 two hours after I had been
handed a letter by Bobby Fasken terminating my employment with
HIDB in four days' time, of which more later.

Completing this brief account of the project work I carried
out for the Board was a survey for a walking route from Lochaber
to Skye provoked by the success of the recently opened Pennine
Way, which I named Wade's Way. At a meeting in Edinburgh of
Enterprise Youth where the suggestion was made, Alec Dickson of
Community Service Volunteers offered to help in the development
of such a walking route.

The line I chose and proposed followed General Wade's route
from Ruthven Barracks in Strathspey to Garva Bridge, where a
smaller barrack building remained roofed, sound and empty, then
over Corrieyairack Pass to Fort Augustus, a route used by the
Hydro Electric Board for their main power line and pylons and then
to follow the military road across the hills to join the right of way
past Loch Affric to Kintail and so on to Skye via Glenelg and
Bernera Barracks. This proposed route, on which I spoke at a Board
meeting in January, was accepted as worth further investigation and
I arranged to meet Scottish Landowners Federation representatives
in March to pursue the idea.

Chapter Four
Moray Firth Development

IN WHAT was to follow it seems important to make clear my family connections in Easter Ross. Subsequent to a war at sea described in *The Führer Led but We Overtook Him*, the submarine I commanded, **HMS Scorcher,** was sent to Invergordon to act as a target for RAF Sunderland flying boats based in the Cromarty Firth. There I met and next year married a farmer's daughter, Jane Paterson, whose parents owned and farmed Ord Farm, Invergordon. Her Father, W G Paterson, a Lovat Scout who had won an MC at Gallipoli, was a splendid tall slim 60 year old golden eagle of a man who, in addition to farming the 360 acre Ord Farm behind the village of Saltburn, also rented and farmed another 400 acres on higher ground. Ord was one of the two arable farms soon to be under threat of compulsory purchase for the establishment of a proposed petro-chemical complex and associated electricity generating plant. These farms, on flat ground accessible to the deep water port of Invergordon, comprised land in the very rare and fertile Capability Classes One and Two.

Thus, in any argument about the destruction of such land rather than siting industry on higher altitude poor quality land a mile further inland, I could fairly be accused of having an interest in the outcome, though certainly not a financial one since every acre of farmland zoned for industrial use was likely to quadruple in value. My father-in-law, for the avoidance of inheritance tax on his death, had in 1962 transferred the ownership of Ord jointly to his son and daughter, my wife.

While working part-time for HIDB, I was one of a small number of staff to become increasingly concerned at the way the private financial interests of at least one Board member was to become too closely linked to its activities. In its first three months of operation, the Board members and staff were occupied in producing a framework to support its activities. To examine and process applications for financial assistance and decide whether help should be offered or not, a grant and loan section, chaired by John Rollo, was established to make recommendations what help, if any, was to be offered. Reports of all visits and meetings were produced, numbered and made available at the monthly plenary meetings. Secretariat papers were also produced to allow the Board to consider its policy over various suggestions and requests for action from MPs and other organisations operating in the Region.

Sadly, on 22nd January 1966, the newly established Board suffered a serious loss when Willie Logan, its highly respected part-time member, tragically lost his life in a plane crash. Thus it was that, on 10th March, Frank Thomson, newly appointed by Willie Ross the Secretary of State for Scotland, attended his first Board meeting. Thomson, already co-director with Colin Campbell of at least eight Polyscot companies and of Invergordon Chemical Enterprises, was promoting an American controlled petro-chemical complex at Invergordon, as described in the extract from the Vigilante minutes which ends Chapter Two of this record.

At this meeting, under the heading Invergordon Development in the minutes, Thomson reported Invergordon Chemical Enterprise's progress in this venture. With him he brought the £55,000 Proplan study he had commissioned as Managing Director of Invergordon Distillers into possible ways to use the CO_2 discharged into the air as a by-product of their whisky production. This study by Dr Jonathan Jenkins had discovered two revolutionary chemical processes which could use this wasted gas. It was only later that the Board discovered that Invergordon Distillers had only so far paid £17,500 towards the cost of this survey. HIDB now commissioned Proplan to prepare a Credibility Study into development in the Moray Firth area at a cost of £4,000. The meeting agreed that the Chairman, Thomson and Dr Jenkins representing Proplan should meet oil interests in London and that consultants should be appointed to investigate the generation of cheap electricity. In May an application for financial help to Polyscot (Polycast) Ltd resulted in a HIDB building grant of £1,500 (unusual as the building was already in use) and a low interest loan of £23,500 being made (£25,000 was the maximum expenditure the Board was allowed to make without consulting St Andrews House).

Dealing with the extensive area of responsibility, stretching from the Mull of Kintyre on the Clyde to Muckle Flugga in Shetland, required extensive travelling by land, sea and air by Board members and staff. All these travel arrangements were handled by locally based travel agent Duncan Duffy of Inverness. Thomson soon invested £40,000 in this firm to become Chairman, Duncan Duffy remaining Managing Director. Reference to Invergordon Development was amended in Board minutes to the more general Moray Firth Development.

In the spring of 1966 Jane became pregnant and, in July, gall bladder trouble was diagnosed and she was admitted for an operation to Raigmore Hospital, then still in wartime wooden huts. While she was recovering in her hospital room, in burst Frank Thomson bearing an enormous 'over the top' bouquet of flowers. He settled down beside her bed and explained the exciting economic potential about to open up in Invergordon. Jane was told there would be an important place for me in the future development and was asked to let me know and confirm I was interested. After he had left it became more and more apparent to her that my strong views on the importance of retaining in agriculture the best arable

45

land on which the future of large stretches of the poorer marginal and hill land depended, and also my family connections with Ord farm were unhelpful to the complex plan. Next day when I visited her we both agreed to do all we could to prevent development taking place on such land.

In 1963, when the 500 acre farm of Kincraig, lying a mile north of Invergordon, came on the market, eight Easter Ross farmers had combined to buy it. The purchase included a large ugly Victorian mansion house and several farm cottages in addition to the farm house. Polyscot group and Invergordon Chemical Enterprise had later rented the big house as an office for one year before Frank Thomson was allowed to join the partnership; with a deed signed that he would purchase it, a cottage and eight acres of land for £15,000, to be paid on 29th November 1966 and based on this deed, the National Commercial Bank made a short-term loan to Easter Ross Farmers to be repaid on that date.

Proplan's Credibility Study became available in August for discussion at HIDB's September meeting, at which John Robertson was relieved of his agricultural and forestry development responsibilities by Prophet Smith, leaving him in charge of Moray Firth Development, assisted by FG Thomson on the Moray Firth project 'including liaison with Invergordon Chemical Enterprises'. Thus Thomson was to liaise with himself. This meeting was attended by Mr Willis, Minister of State for Scotland, where Dr Jenkins talked of how his Credibility Study had emphasised the importance of cheap electrical power in attracting industry, suggesting that the possibility of a gas turbine plant fuelled from the petro-chemical complex should be studied in more detail. Thus Government could not complain it was unaware of the investigations HIDB was carrying out. The Board at this meeting agreed to maintain details of all monies expended on the development of the petro-chemical complex "in order that company formation expenses could be allocated at a later date". Heads I win, tails you lose as far as Thomson was concerned. When a fee to

Proplan was agreed, John Rollo is minuted as remarking that no
details of the survey application had been made available.

On 11th October, Grieve, Robertson, Thomson, Jenkins and
Fasken, HIDB's Secretary, travelled to Claridge's Hotel where they
met Dr Armand Hammer and four other company executives. Hammer
confirmed that Occidental Oil intended to pursue the Invergordon
project and that he accepted the arrangements outlined by Mr
Thomson, who spoke for HIDB at the meeting. He was promised that
suitable arable land was available at a cost of £200 to £300 an acre. At
that time good arable land was selling for at least £200 an acre, so land
for industrial development was being offered at little more than its
agricultural price. Professor Grieve then gave the following
assurances: the Government would give a 40% investment grant on
plant and machinery and a 35% building grant. He said the proposal
for a Government loan of half the balance of costs remaining was
reasonable and this, together with a possible moratorium on interest
and capital payments, would form part of the discussions on the
Government loan. Both sides agreed to meet again in America in
November. By now the fee to Proplan for Dr Jenkins's work was £50 a
day, considerably more than Professor Grieve was paid.

It is time to introduce our close friend Dr Ian Grimble,
Highland historian, author, broadcaster on the Third Programme
and ex-House of Commons librarian, who was to play a crucial role
in what was to become the Highland Board row, alternatively
described as 'the Durham affair'. Ian, an ex Westminster School
classmate and friend of Anthony Wedgwood Benn, shared a house
with an eccentric painter at Bettyhill on the north coast of
Sutherland and was Chairman of Caithness and Sutherland Labour
Party, whose young candidate Robert Maclennan, a lawyer, had in
1964 been elected MP. With a remarkable linguistic facility, Ian had
been a Japanese translator on Mountbatten's staff at SEAC
headquarters in Kandy and later Delhi, and subsequently added
Gaelic to his many languages. I had discussed my concern, shared
by several other workers in HIDB's office, about Moray Firth

Development with Ian. On 25th October Ian wrote a memorandum on Frank Thomson's involvement therein. This memorandum detailed the Polyscot deficit, its grant and loan from HIDB in May and application for a further loan in August, and the approval of a fee for producing draft hotel plans, such a fee being unavailable to others making competitive proposals, and the substantial payments made to Proplan. By then it had become clear that Invergordon Chemical Enterprises was to be the main beneficiary of all the preliminary work for the petro-chemical complex carried out and paid for by HIDB. Copies of this memorandum were sent to both Wedgwood Benn, then Minister of Technology in the Cabinet, and Robert Maclennan. By now a small team led by Frank Spaven, chief planning and research officer of HIDB, was set up to liaise with Douglas Fasken, ex Sutherland County Development Officer, who had resigned to work for Invergordon Chemical Enterprises.

The ever increasing staff of HIDB had seriously outgrown the accommodation available in its headquarters behind Inverness Library and in a rented house half a mile away, so I had been instructed to do as much of my work as possible at home, using a tape recorder to dictate letters for typing later; when I did work in Inverness there was usually a vacant office available to use. Thus I gathered copies of all the Board's minutes, notes of visits, secretariat papers and my various research and correspondence files on seed potato export, possible establishment of Wade's Way and youth activities and took them home to Scotsburn. While some of the more sensitive notes of Moray Firth Development meetings were kept out of general files all were successively numbered and referred to in HIDB meeting agendas which made it comparatively easy to discover what was afoot. At this time early in December at Ian Grimble's suggestion I started to keep a diary whose first entries were to note that, to the discomfort of the partners in Easter Ross Farmers, Thomson's cheque of £15,000 to pay for the house, cottage and land did not arrive on 29th November as promised; and also of press reports of an attack in the *Scotsman* by Lord Lovat on

Grieve and the Board, claiming it was time they gave an account of their activities as it was widely believed they were concentrating more on tourism than the interests of Highland people.

A repeated request for a grant and loan of £25,000 as working capital for Ross-Shire Engineering in Dingwall, a firm rescued from liquidation by Thomson and others, was due to come up for decision the second time in mid-December. The Secretariat had repeated a recommendation this application be refused.

In the office John Rollo told me that Grieve was beginning to have doubts about Thomson who had hardly participated in the American talks and, when they asked where the British participating cash was to come from, he did not as usual claim he could raise it. We discussed the value of the agricultural land needed and I said I thought £1,000 an acre was realistic.

When John Robertson returned from Montreal the week before HIDB's Plenary Meeting on 15th December, Frank Thomson did not accompany him but stayed in the States till the day before the meeting, on the conclusion of which he, grey-faced, told me he had bronchitis and was taking both penicillin and aureomycin. When, investigating electricity generating costs, he had visited Tennessee Valley Authority with its extensive hydro-electric generation along the dammed Colorado River, he had been told they were conservative in their electricity policy but had received four times as much from industrialists as they had spent to attract it. That evening, at the meeting of the Consultative Council Education Sub Committee, a long discussion of the queries raised in my report on youth activities resulted in agreement with my main claim that they were inseparably linked to the Government's and Local Authorities' educational policies.

By this time the County Clerk of Ross & Cromarty County Council had called a meeting, attended by planning and development officials and members of the NFU, to consider the land needed for industrial development. The HIDB note of this meeting began "This meeting was of mysterious origin". At it Reay

Clarke, the local NFU Chairman, after being told by the Board representative present that it was not possible to provide details of the proposed petro-chemical development, gave the terms of a prepared press release by the NFU emphasising farmers' support for industrial development provided it was sited off the scarce top quality agricultural land. Eventually he was persuaded not to release this statement, reserving the right to release it later should this appear appropriate. Instead a bland joint press release was agreed and issued, to be completely disregarded by the press. However it was very clear to HIDB that farmers would not relinquish the best land without a fight.

Next morning at nine I was phoned at home by a member of HIDB staff who, in an urgent voice, warned me there was a hell of a flap in the office because some document had got into the hands of a Cabinet member, not the Scottish Secretary. So Ian's memo had reached Tony Benn. Later, when I was next in the Board's office, it was mentioned to me by my informant that I had been rung up on John Rollo's instruction and I was then further warned that it had been decided to plant papers in the office in an endeavour to catch the person concerned.

December had been a month of torrential rain which had filled to overflowing the Hydro Electric Board's dams over the headwaters of the Conon river. Thus, when Jane and I at lunch heard on the one o'clock news that a flood alert for Conon village and A9 had been issued, we decided, with the birth of our third child imminent, I had better drive her to Raigmore Hospital in Inverness at once. After crossing the river bridge into Conon, the river had already overflowed to flood the basement of the Conon Hotel and water on the road was already lapping the car wheels. Once she was safely settled in hospital, I set off home in darkness to discover a hundred yards of road in Conon under water. Driving boldly into the flood, it was only when water started to flood my feet through the foot pedals and my shoes filled with water that I appreciated its depth. Inevitably the engine stalled and I was stuck till firemen in thigh waders splashed up to push the car on to higher dry ground beside the bridge. Remarkably, after quarter of an hour's wait, the engine spluttered into juddering life with three cylinders firing. After waiting for a few more minutes in the hope the plugs might dry off, I let in the clutch and managed to judder the twenty miles home again. Thirty six hours later I was phoned to be told of the safe arrival of a son and that mother and son ought to be home for Christmas four days later.

Before then, at the Board's second Christmas party, John Robertson button-holed me to inquire about recent NFU activities as he had missed the last two quarterly meetings and had been told Frank Thomson had been involved in a row with Douglas Budge and his Kincraig partnership. I explained that I had heard that a promised cheque had failed to arrive which was causing them embarrassment with their bankers.

On 27th December the petro chemical complex proposal featured under the headline "It's a real Highland fling" an article quoting Professor Grieve as stating 'before it comes to the point of utilising farmland for industry, housing and other facilities, there will be the fullest consultation'. That day Colin Campbell told Reay Clarke that NFU Invergordon publicity had been most unfortunate in its timing and, as I ate my lunchtime sandwich in the Board office, John Robertson came into the room and settled down. We chatted about seed potato export where, as a result of my survey, RTS potatoes, in which as landlord he had declared an interest, had been awarded a £7,500 loan to operate a potato handling plant in the wartime mine filling shed he owned. We also discussed my ideas for the possible Wade's Way walking route.

The phone rang: it was Bill from St Andrews House discussing power stations. John remarked that he had heard that Wedgwood Benn, minister of Technology, was interested in the development of small power stations sited alongside the industries they were to supply, and he thought it very important to get the Minister's support for Invergordon as such a site. He felt every effort should be made to involve this young and influential minister. After putting the phone down, he said he was worried about the NFU reaction when Kelloggs visited farms for exploratory drilling in the New Year. He indicated that by using powers of compulsion it would be possible to obtain farm land at existing use value and quoted an Easter Ross farm recently sold at £126 an acre. He said he could not understand why the farmers were not supporting the Board. I replied the reason was both their neglect of agriculture and their failure to make their plans known despite constant leaks in the press. When he claimed that they could not tell people the firm involved as it was too confidential, I replied that opposition would continue and indeed intensify till the Board did declare themselves and suggested he might at least as a start approach the NFU president, Reay Clarke in confidence.

John next turned to discussing the price of land. He thought £200 an acre too low if freely negotiated and claimed the NFU guff about good arable land not being used was purely to force up the price and that price was the sole criterion. I replied he was quite wrong. He next asked me how much the farmers wanted? To this I mentioned that £1,000 an acre was recently agreed at Dunfermerline to which he retorted this was utter nonsense. Surely they'd settle for £500 an acre, after all, if they reinvested in another farm, capital gains would not be payable. He quoted land in Caithness selling at £30 to £40 an acre. Then came the punchline: should farmers fail to agree a reasonable price, the Board would publicly attack them and publish their names as the guilty men who, by opposing Highland development, would be responsible for wrecking the future prosperity of the area. He went on to admit that failure to agree a price would probably wreck the American petro-chemical complex plan which could not be delayed, but threatened that then compulsory purchase procedure would at once be instigated to acquire the land for other industrial use, and that every possible step would be taken to keep the price down to existing use value. I made no further comment and John left the room.

Chapter Five
Ultimatum

ON NEW Year's Eve John spent some time at the Polyscot office in Kincraig House with Frank before travelling to Edderton to visit Reay, there to repeat the talk he had earlier had with me. He did for the first time admit that no British participation (apart from Government) in the complex was likely. Reay agreed to call a special meeting of the Easter Ross NFU executive committee early in the New Year to meet John, who would also be given an opportunity to address the forthcoming area AGM on 20th January about the proposed development. He emphasised to Reay his hope that there would be no compulsory purchase and that, while he believed the District Valuer would propose £130 an acre, the Board might even double this or, just possibly, go as far as £400 an acre for an agreed sale.

With rumours rife, an NFU sub committee entitled the Easter Ross Land Use Committee, made up of the farmers around Invergordon, and chaired by Reay from outside the area, had been convened and taken the decision that, only when HIDB agreed to commission a proper professional land capability study, would access to members farms be granted to the American consultants Kelloggs to carry out borings. After appointing solicitors and agreeing an opening subscription of £20 a farm they agreed to accept an offer of co-operation from Invergordon Distillers, who were concerned by the possible effect an adjoining petro-chemical complex might have on maturing stocks of whisky. Douglas Budge, the chairman of Kincraig Farmers, told the meeting about the problem their members faced from their bankers as a result of Thomson breaking a legal commitment.

At this time HIDB's newly formed Moray Firth Development Committee began to liaise with Kelloggs Consultants and discuss permitted levels of pollution with the Ministry of Technology. The decisions of this committee, which included the development and planning officers of Ross & Cromarty County Council, were later to lead to them resigning when their advice was either over-ruled or disregarded. When the Jack Holmes Planning Group were appointed they also joined this committee, and took over planning in the Moray Firth area.

In a cabinet reshuffle George Willis was replaced by Dr Dickson Mabon as Minister of State at the Scottish Office and Grieve, Robertson and Thomson were bidden to Edinburgh to meet top civil servants Sir Matthew Campbell and Sir Douglas Haddow. There, I was told, the speech Robertson was to make to Ross & Cromarty County Council's 18th January meeting was vetted and amended before receiving Scottish Office approval. When he made a quite different speech from the embargoed copy issued to the Press, they complained at having to rewrite their prepared articles.

By then I had informed Ian Grimble of Thomson's failure to pay the promised £15,000 to Kincraig Farmers and, having become aware that Lord Strathclyde, Chairman of the North of Scotland Hydro-Electric Board, was about to attend an Inverness meeting which was to consider an application that Frank Thomson join its membership, I typed a memorandum on his activities in Invergordon Chemical Enterprises and elsewhere to make clear my belief in the undesirability of appointing him to the Hydro Board. Through a cousin, Sybil Paterson, and a local solicitor member of the Hydro Board who shared local concern, this was passed to Lord Strathclyde in advance of the meeting. Later the press was to report that Lord Lovat at dead of night had tiptoed along a corridor of the Station Hotel in Inverness and slipped it under Strathclyde's bedroom door. The Highland grapevine is far too effective to require any such manoeuvres.

The day after John's address to the County Council which led to such headlines as "It's Invergolden" and "2,000 jobs on the way", I was called up to the Highland boardroom to report on my suggestions for Wade's Way. I was authorised to spend up to £1,000 in continued research and consultation with landowners, local authorities and amenity bodies.

When everyone had left the Board's office for lunch, wandering around the building, I discovered piled beside the photo-copier the pages of the secret HIDB 28 meeting minute which committed the Board to pursuing the petro-chemical project as its main target against any opposition it might have to face. I removed one sheet from the top of each pile. At last it was clear the extent of the Government's grant aid promised by HIDB on its behalf to the American company Occidental Oil. I also read that day two reports made by Proplan, one of fertiliser distribution in Britain and the other headed 'Mix survey'. That night on return home I drafted and typed well into the night the eight foolscap page memorandum soon to be delivered into the hands of the Minister of State by a young Highland Labour MP. (see Appendix)

I sent my information and a covering letter to Ian Grimble who replied *"I have just received your letter and enclosures which I will hand over to Robert this evening when we meet. Robert had already met Mabon but did not get instant satisfaction and is keeping his right of access to William Ross in reserve."* Robert Maclennan, who the year before had been elected Labour MP for Caithness & Sutherland, was to serve as messenger between the North and Westminster, encouraged by the Chairman of his local party, Ian Grimble.

Four days later, when we decided early resolution of the situation was needed, after a phone discussion Ian wrote *"I handed*

*your fortnight's ultimatum to Robert yesterday afternoon. He
approved of it and may have passed it already to the Secretary of
State. He has already spoken to William Ross who said rather airily
that all the facts were in his possession. I also saw Wedgwood Benn
yesterday with Robert who later phoned to say he hoped to see you
at the weekend."*

At the Easter Ross NFU AGM, John Robertson was given a
courteous hearing, though members were surprised at his reference
to "our American partners". He announced that 300 acres of land
would be required for the initial industrialisation and said the
Americans would receive exactly the same government assistance
as anyone else in a development area – no more and no less.
Prophet Smith, who also attended, did not speak. John stated other
companies, some of them British, were also interested.

Two days later on Saturday, 28th January the *Scotsman*
published an article including a letter from Miss Jean Forsyth, who
lived at Balintraid Farm marching with Ord to the East, under the
heading 'Simply nothing here but fields'. Below is the article
which so well expressed the anxieties of the farming community at
what they regarded as HIDB's mistaken neglect of the value of rare
arable land in the Region.

"'Let's face it, we must bring industry into the Borders,
there's simply nothing here but fields.' This conversational remark
was made recently by an industrialist referring to the Scottish
Border country.

"It could at a stretch, be equally applied to the Scottish
Highlands and, according to Miss Jean E Forsyth of Balintraid,
Delny, Ross-shire, the sentiment expressed in the remark would
seem to be the same as the attitude taken by the chairman and the
members of the Highlands and Islands Development Board.

"She claims that the Board lays sweeping claim to the whole
of the Moray Firth area as being suitable for development. This
apparently arrogant claim is, she believes, due to a lack of
knowledge of land and the ecology thereof.

"In a letter to *The Scotsman*, Miss Forsyth writes:– *I must point out to the Board that the land which looks so nice and easy to lay out with roads, factories and houses is, in fact, already highly developed. This land has been cultivated for centuries as a food producing factory which never wears out or depreciates, so long as it is treated under the laws of good husbandry; it is a national asset that must never be destroyed.*

"The farm from which I write is situated near Invergordon, and is of a group of farms threatened by destruction in the interests of what the Board refer to as development. They wish to make this land available for the erection of a petro-chemical plant to be built by an American firm on behalf of an American company.

"Presumably this company will be trading in opposition to our petroleum companies of the same type. I do not understand the economic thinking behind a plan which would put valuable agricultural land plus its native owners out of business for the sake of foreigners who are trade competitors.

"The food that will no longer be grown here will have to be grown elsewhere. Has this fact been taken into account by the chairman of the Board? I am anxious to know has he taken the elementary step of ascertaining the amount of primary food and seed potatoes that would be lost annually per acre by destroying this land, and how far forward he has projected the loss.

"This is the procedure that comes under the heading of long-term planning, and is absolutely essential before any fundamental change is allowed to come about in the economic and social structure of a county such as this.

"The acreage of unproductive land here is enormous compared with the small quantity of cultivated ground, mostly on the East Coast fringe. Any tampering with the low ground would immediately lead to an imbalance of the farming structure of the county as a whole.

"The hill cattle and sheep come to the low farms for wintering and fattening; so that every acre of good ground lost

means fewer cattle and sheep from the hill, less food for a rising population.

"The Highlands and Islands Development Board was brought into being to help the crofter counties to adjust to present-day economic trends and to make the best use of its natural assets, or so I imagined, but I could be wrong.

"If my first assumption is correct, how is it that one of its first attempts at development will lead to the displacement of native farm businesses which have served themselves and their country well over several generations? The farmers I refer to are as progressive and forward looking as any in Scotland, and are backed by staffs of adaptable and skilled men. The land they cultivate, and the skill they use in doing so, are national assets which cannot be lightly thrown aside, no matter how glittering the short-term material gain might appear.

"If I am wrong in my understanding of the Board's reason for existence, I presume that the native Highlanders will just become pawns in a game of economic power politics with little or no say in their own destiny. This, I regret to write, is the feeling I have at this tense moment in the life of Easter Ross. I would gladly have it dispelled, but by whom?

"My lack of confidence in the Board is, I believe, due to the Act of Parliament which set it up. This gave too great moral and executive responsibility to appointed men; the responsibility of great legal power and the power of money; the power of private patronage and public punishment.

"By public punishment I mean what could so easily happen to owners or tenants of land who find themselves in the position of the farmers round Invergordon. If they do not wish to surrender their homes and livelihood to the Board on negotiated terms, but try to defend themselves, what happens next? If they choose not to take the reputedly large sums of money they will be offered by the Board for their farms, but choose to continue their almost profitless task of food production, because they are doing the job they were

trained for and can do no other, will they be held up to public obloquy, and removed by compulsory purchase? Public punishment for what crime?

"By public patronage I mean the large sums of money expended in grants and loans to private persons and businesses. There is too much secrecy about these operations. Quite large sums are mentioned as single loans and I think the public should know what are the priorities laid down for grants and loans, also the conditions under which people may apply for them.

"I have not seen any published information on this subject such as is provided by other Government Departments. For instance the Department of Agriculture gives a great variety of grants which are advertised or published in booklet form, so that the applicant or any interested person can see the size and condition of grant.

"Why does not the Board do likewise? It would help to stop some of the uneasy, and probably misinformed, gossip on this subject one hears from time to time.

"I hope I have managed to indicate something of the strain and bewilderment to which the people in the North have suddenly become subject. They are the victims of an experimental form of government that could have tragic consequences. Their traditional form of local government, with their representatives elected by popular vote, is becoming subject to a form of powerful bureaucratic government.

"I do not believe this was intended to happen: I believe the democratic principle was accidentally omitted in the Act of Parliament which brought the new form of government into being.

"The position that has arisen is that there is an entirely new government department sitting in Inverness, manned by a large body of civil servants, and managed by a board appointed by the Government in power, not by democratic vote. I refer to the Highlands and Islands Development Board.

The local county councils and town councils, spread as they are over the whole of the crofter counties with their small staffs of public servants can never, in fact, oppose the Board.

"In theory, yes, but in fact what hope have they against a large staff grouped together in one office with plenty of money to spend on plans, while the county council official is prevented from doing a small necessary survey because of the credit squeeze? What hope have our council members to stand up to the plans and predictions of "experts", backed by dazzling figures and graphs, etc, which are the weapons of the people with a vested interest in planning? I guess the answer is that they will just be bowled over.

"There is a dilemma to be resolved in the Highlands: democratic government or bureaucratic government? The answer to this question will, I believe, have an effect far beyond the bounds of this beautiful – and vulnerable – country."

The day the *Scotsman* article was published, but not circulated in Tom Johnson's press cuttings of items which might be of interest to Board members and staff, I was away at a meeting held in Edinburgh by Enterprise Youth Scotland attended by Judith Hart, a Government minister, where Professor Grieve spoke about my idea of a Highland walking route and said Community Service Volunteers were keen to help in its establishment. As a result I was phoned next day by the *Guardian* and, a day later, by most Scottish papers about the idea and route. Slightly to my embarrassment James Laing of the *Scottish Daily Mail* wrote a long article rather more about me than my ideas for Wade's Way headed "A man who is putting his heart in the Highlands": unfortunate timing as it turned out. I discovered I should have referred all press enquiries to Jimmy Grassie, the Board's publicity officer. Once more I seemed to have upset civil service protocol.

When I was next in the Board office, John Rollo came down to tell me that, on 29th December prior to the Invergordon Chemical Enterprises/Moray Firth Development submission going off to the Secretary of State, he had seen Sir Matthew Campbell to say he intended to resign, only to be told he must do no such thing, and that the scheme had not been approved by the Secretary of State who had already informed Grieve and Fasken that no government assistance would be available until it had been approved as viable by the Ministry of Economic Affairs, the Board of Trade and the Ministry of Technology. Were Kellogs to advise Occidental to proceed and Government then not agree, there was real likelihood the Americans would demand their £150,000 back. Sir Matthew Campbell had said this was not the right sort of development for the Highlands to which Grieve had replied: "I do not agree, we'll never sort the Highland problem by pissing against a wall". When, at the weekend, Grieve, Robertson and Smith met members of the Northern Pastoral Club, Lord Lovat concluded an attacking speech to say Robertson had now clearly become an enemy of the entire farming community: John went very white showing severe discomfort. The Board had just advertised the post of land use officer and, amongst the applicants for the job was Reay Clarke who appeared eminently well qualified for it but was not eventually chosen.

My fortnight's ultimatum expired on 9th February with neither visit nor phone call from Robert Maclennan. That day I received a letter from Ian. He wrote *"I will be speaking to Robert before I finish this letter and will ask him to return the copy of Proplan's Credibility Study you lent him at once. What I am not supposed to tell you but I will now do since he did not see you. He was initially delighted you were going to feed the whole story to the press. Everyone, he thought, had been given his chance and now needed prodding by exposure and agitation. I agree. But then he saw Oor Wullie who told him TOP SECRET that he proposed to get rid of Frank Thomson but could not be hustled into anything so delicate. Robert intended to propose to you the moratorium be extended. I am not sure that any further delay could be justified. I have now made up my mind and hope you will at once publish and be damned. Please remember that it is Robert who has put the right case to the right people, running grave risks to his career right at the outset in this."*

Here I found myself keen to "publish and be damned"
without any idea how to do so. The *Sunday Times* Insight team
seemed the ideal destination but how to reach them? I found a
friend to give the bare bones of my concern to Antony Vice, who
had just moved from the Insight team to become business editor of
the *Times*: he asked for details so, after obtaining an explicit
assurance on confidentiality, I sent him a copy of the memorandum
which had earlier been passed to the Secretary of State. Two days
later a Mr Casement from the *Times* rang to ask to see copies of the
original HIDB documents to which I had referred in my
memorandum. Reluctantly I sent them off by recorded delivery
and, four days later, he phoned me to say that a 1,500 to 2,000
word article would appear in the following Saturday's *Times*, but
nothing appeared on 18th February, the day all the Scottish papers
reported the installation of Frank Thomson as Rector of Aberdeen
University. Both Grieve and John Dailey representing Dr Hammer,
President of Occidental Oil who was that day meeting the King of
Morocco, attended the ceremony. The *Press & Journal* leader was
headed "Modern Rector". John Rollo had already warned me that
Thomson's one hope would be a successful libel or slander action
to stifle criticism.

When I finally managed to talk on the phone to Casement late
on Sunday night, he informed me that he had spoken to John
Robertson who, possibly accompanied by Frank Thomson, would
visit the *Times* office on Wednesday. He emphasised to me that
Thomson was a known millionaire and that his connection with a
skeleton company was not strong evidence. I was appalled: so
much for confidentiality.

That afternoon Reay Clarke in his Edderton home was visited
for tea by Thomson accompanied by John Dailey who told him
that, should Thomson be killed in a car crash, Occidental would
probably withdraw as their confidence was in him and not in the
Highland Board. Frank had approached them, found the site, and

done everything for them and they were grateful as this does not normally happen. After Reay had rung up to tell of this, I spoke to Ian who agreed to visit the *Times* office next day to retrieve the papers I had sent them. There, after being kept waiting, he collected them back, revealing to Casement who he and Maclennan were.

I was later told that the Editor of the *Times,* who had been shown my memorandum, was so concerned by its contents and its implications that he had contacted Lord Astor, the paper's proprietor, whose approach to Government led to an agreement to suppress it and, instead, print a laudatory centre page article supporting HIDB's heavy industrial hopes.

Now that the Government's documents have been released under the 30-year rule, it is possible to quote what Bobby Fasken, the Board's Secretary, reported to St Andrew's House at that time (file SEP 12/560). On 27th February he referred to a leak of confidential documents to the *Times*. *"The* Times *journalist (Mr Roy Mackie) had, in fact, just transferred from the* Sunday Times *and but for these changes there might well have been publication of an article deploying the information and the criticism which, it was understood, had accompanied it. Mr John Robertson made contact with the editor of the* Times *(Mr Rees-Mogg) and arranged to meet him and Mr Mackie in London last Wednesday (22nd February). From this meeting it became clear that the* Times *indeed had photostat copies of a number of confidential papers, and they also had a five-page memorandum by someone rehearsing the transactions regarding projects with which Mr Thomson had some connection. Mr Robertson emphasised that these disclosures must have been made in breach of the Official Secrets Act, that the disclosure represented a dangerous and poisonous attack on the Board and particularily one of its members, with which, he would have thought, the* Times *would not wish to be associated. Indeed he pressed that the* Times *should instead publish a constructive article dealing with the Board and its work and, in particular, the Invergordon project, and putting the 'whispering campaign' into perspective. This suggestion was accepted, and the outcome was the article in the* Times *on Saturday, 25th February, featuring the Board and 'the £150m. Highland Fling' acknowledging the criticisms that were being made, particularly against Mr Thomson, but making it clear that the 1965 Act made provision for the Board assisting enterprises with which particular Board members might be associated, and repeating the Board's assurances that all the procedures were properly observed. The editor of the* Sunday Times *has subsequently given an assurance to Prof. Grieve that he will not publish anything without first consulting Prof. Grieve and giving him an opportunity to state the Board's position and views, so as to ensure a balanced article.*

I discovered next day when working in the Board's office that Robertson and a Mr Rossitor of Merz & Maclennan had, without prior notice or permission, walked over Inverbreakie and Ord Farms to plan where to bore to investigate the underlying rock. The next time I worked in HIDB's office was Friday, 24th February, ready to attend the Consultative Council Education Sub-committee meeting that evening. At 5.20 p.m. Bobby Fasken came downstairs to hand me a letter marked Personal which, when I opened it, stated:–

"As part of the re-organisation of Board staff now in process of implementation the Board has decided the time has come to discontinue temporary and part time appointments to their staff.

I accordingly regret I have to give you formal notice of the termination on 28th February, 1967 of your temporary part time appointment with the Board.

Would you please sign the attached Declaration under the Official Secrets Act? In terms of Section 5 of this Declaration I should be glad if you would return all sketches, plans, models, articles, files, notes or documents, together with all drafts or copies of the same which you have acquired or made during the term of your appointment with the Board.

These should be returned to me personally by registered post

together with the enclosed certificate duly signed.
    Yours sincerely, (R.A. Fasken) Secretary."

Before the evening meeting in the Board office I discovered a copy of a proposed harbour plan for Invergordon which involved taking over the Admiralty pier. Believing this would be of interest to a friend, Vice Admiral Sir John Hayes who, as flag officer for Scotland and Northern Ireland was responsible for the dockyard, piers and oil fuel depot, I sent a copy to Rosyth.

At the meeting I heard that the first annual report of HIDB would be available for discussion at their next meeting at the end of March. Events were about to dictate otherwise.

On the same day that I had been given my four day's notice, Jane was rung up by Lord Lovat who agreed to meet her secretly in a wood five miles from Scotsburn. After discovering how well informed he was she, without inquiring just how he had discovered with whom to get in touch, invited him to come and meet me two days later. Before then almost half the centre page of the *Times* bore the bold article by Roy Mackie below photographs of Grieve, Rollo, Robertson and Thomson headed "The £150m Highland Fling". It later became known that much of the substance of the article had actually been supplied by John Robertson, typed in the Board's office and delivered to the *Times*. Its first paragraph read *"The recent outflow of confidential information from the Inverness offices of the Highlands and Islands Development Board has been ruthlessly stopped"*. So, the *Times* knew of my sacking before I did. The *Times's* revelation of the source of the information I gave them and publication of this article disregarding it surely contributed to the vigorous press publicity which followed.

Dealing with Thomson's interest the article stated *"There is suspicion that Thomson will be the main beneficiary if the petrochemical complex gets going. It is true he has a substantial interest in Invergordon Chemical Enterprise which will probably be the shell that will carry the scheme but he registered that company years ago... and he assured the Board that this will be available to them to use as a vehicle on their terms".*

In fact it had only been registered in November 1965, less than sixteen months earlier, while his assurance to the Board had no legal validity and was meaningless.

By the time Lovat arrived at Scotsburn, Ian had visited the *Sunday Express* with the story of the *Times* betrayal and soon found himself ushered into the presence of its editor, John Gordon. Thus it was that he rang me up to talk to me while Lovat was with us, questioning me closely before telling me that his assistant editor, John Junor, later to replace him and, like him, to be knighted, would be in touch early in the week. He would first speak to Max Rayne of London Merchant Securities who owned Invergordon Distillers to find out why Thomson had been replaced. Jane and I were surprised how well informed Lovat was. When we had discussed the situation, he phoned his brother Hugh, Tory MP and past Secretary of State for Air, putting him in touch with Ian Grimble, Labour Constituency Party Chairman: it seemed to have become a cross party concern.

The *Glasgow Herald* next morning published the first of three articles by John Kerr on the petro chemical complex plan entitled "Mini clearances at Invergordon" which examined the difficulties of the farmers of Easter Ross, uncertain of their future. As I read it, James Laing from the *Scottish Daily Mail* rang up to say he knew there was the hell of a row in HIDB's office and he wanted to know what it was. He offered to come up if I'd talk to him and, despite my replying I could not, he came north in any case.

That day, three days after my dismissal notice was handed to me, at Sunday lunch with my in-laws at Ord, my brother-in-law asked me if anyone else had been sacked. He had heard about it from the manager of Scottish Agricultural industries store in Invergordon. Ian Grimble who had spent the day in London with Hugh Fraser rang up to let us know that Max Rayne had talked to the editor of the *Times* and that by now both he and the Secretary of

State, Willie Ross, were aware they were on the wrong side. He had also had a long discussion with John Junor of the *Sunday Express*.

Before James Laing returned to Glasgow on the Monday, after at our suggestion making a round of visits in Easter Ross, when he rang to say goodbye, he told Jane it was rumoured I'd been given four days' notice expiring that night. I told him I was sorry I could not speak. I mentioned the Official Secrets Act threat which he suggested was nonsense in a matter like this. That afternoon Jane attended a meeting of the Easter Ross Land Use Committee who refused the offer of its chairman Reay Clarke to resign because he had replied to HIDB's advertisement of the job of land use officer. He informed the meeting that the County Council proposed on 10th March to amend the County Development Plan to zone Inverbreakie and Ord farms for industrial use and that thereafter a public inquiry seemed inevitable. The Committee decided to approach Hunting Technical Services to carry out a land capability survey of members' land and to seek a share of the cost from HIDB. They also agreed to invite members of the County Council to visit the farms concerned.

The next visitor to arrive at Scotsburn on Thursday was Peter Vane of the *Sunday Express*. Having been frostily received when he had called at the Board's office, he landed with us for supper and was still here when a car drew up at the front door and the driver handed me a letter. It read:-

3rd March, 1967
Dear Sir,
        I am directed to deliver to you the enclosed statement which has this evening been communicated to the Times *in response to an approach which that newspaper made to the Board today.*
        Yours faithfully,
        A. E. Mitchell
        Assistant Secretary.

STATEMENT TO *THE TIMES*

Mr P E Durham, a temporary part time member of the Board's staff, was dismissed by the Board on February 28. From evidence gathered from within the Board Mr Durham appeared to have been concerned in passing confidential Board documents to persons outside the Board. Mr Durham has today been so informed."

In case *The Times* were to publish this statement, I did prepare, with Peter Vane's help, my own statement ready for use, but the *Times* remained silent. After my original dismissal letter I had pointed out that I was due a month's notice or wage in lieu and emphasised how important it was that another Board employee should honour the various obligations I had entered into and appointments I had made.

When John Junor rang up he mentioned that their libel lawyers had warned it might be costly to publish my information; however he did not think Thomson could take action against me, as my letter to *The Times* was privileged. He was utterly appalled at the *Times's* action in apparently handing my memorandum to John Robertson. He mentioned that Alasdair Mackenzie had put down two questions to Government for Willie Ross to answer in the House about financial commitments to the proposed petro-chemical development, to which he had not received a proper reply.

Next forenoon, a farmer friend, Sandy Lawson, agreed to alert Gordon Campbell and Tony Stoddart to what was afoot, while Lovat agreed to speak to the Convener of Ross and Cromarty County Council Murdo Nicolson, a free church minister whose nickname (sic) was Nick the Devil. Then, at 3 p.m. Junor rang to say he had spoken about my dismissal to the Editor of *The Times* who told him HIDB claimed I had been dismissed because they had intercepted a phone call of mine. This was untrue; they had spent some time trying to recognise the writing in two disguised and left-hand written amendments made to the typing of my original memorandum brought back from the *Times* office.

What would happen next?

Chapter Six

Out in the open

T HIS IS what John Gordon wrote on Sunday, 5th March
1967 in his Current Events column:–
*"Let us consider today the story of a man, who, for daring
to do what he thought a good citizen should do, found himself
swiftly clobbered by a public body which, like so many similar
bodies, didn't like its affairs being publicly discussed.*

*As the projected spending of more than £100 million of public
money is involved, it seems to me that full disclosure of what is
going on is imperative so that allegations made should be publicly
proved or demolished.*

*The man is Philip Durham, a small hill farmer in the North of
Scotland. As a submariner in the war he won the DSC at 24. After
the war, when commanding a submarine, he contracted polio, lost
the use of his legs, and has since faced life in a wheelchair. When
the Highlands and Islands Development Board was set up 18
months ago he took a part time job with it.*

*The board set about its task with quite exceptional energy
and imagination.*

*In a short time it found itself concerned in schemes which in
one case alone, an industrial project for the Moray Firth region,
involved £100 million.*

Mr Durham came to the conclusion, rightly or wrongly, that public money was being mis-used. He wrote a memorandum of his views and such information as he had, which was handed privately to The Times.

Within a few days of the memorandum reaching The Times *he was abruptly sacked. Before he was sacked a member of the development board paid a visit to the* Times *office. Obviously Mr Durham's identity as a critical employee in contact with a newspaper had leaked.*

But his dismissal letter did not mention that. He was merely told he was redundant. And reminded, perhaps significantly, of his responsibilities under the Official Secrets Act.

Twenty four hours after his dismissal The Times *printed a laudatory article about the Board, in particular praising a man closely associated with the Moray Firth project which Mr Durham had criticised.*

The Sunday Express *checked the coincidence of these events with* The Times. *Then a surprising thing happened. About 10 o'clock on Friday night two Development Board officials arrived at Mr Durham's home with a letter signed by the assistant secretary in the board.*

It said: "I am directed to deliver to you the enclosed statement which has this evening been communicated to The Times *in response to an approach which that newspaper made to the Board today."*

The statement read: "Mr Durham.... was dismissed by the Board on February 28th. From evidence gathered within the Board, Mr Durham appeared to have been concerned in passing confidential documents to persons outside the Board."

Now the vital point is not who gave Mr Durham away to the Board bosses – and I am sure it wasn't the Times *– but why the Board should be so anxious to conceal what goes on in a matter involving so much public money.*

If there is no sound foundation for Mr Durham's criticisms, then obviously the proper course for the board to take is to meet them with a full public refutation. To threaten him with the Official Secrets Act in order to shut him up is a misuse of that Act.

In the interests of all concerned, not least of them the taxpayers who have to find the millions, it is time we were told fully and accurately what goes on,"

We spent the forenoon amending the press statement I had prepared to explain my concern at what was going on. While doing so two car loads of journalists arrived on the front gravel seeking an interview or statement. I told them that a statement would be passed to the Press Association later but, when they rang to tell me they were not prepared to issue it, we regretted sending the cars away. They had left to attend a press conference in Inverness arranged by HIDB. We were later told by a *Scotsman* reporter that there were signs of panic there. As we prepared to ring our statement through to each paper, a *Glasgow Herald* journalist who rang kindly offered to circulate it for us. A local photographer arrived to photograph myself and Jane holding our three-month old baby for the *Press & Journal.* It was not till 7 p.m. that a Mr Warren from *The Times* rang, to receive a frosty reception. I passed my statement with a demand that, should they choose to use it, they published it in full and unamended. Next morning at the bottom of the front page of *The Times* appeared an article justifying my dismissal. John Robertson was stated as pointing out that the Official Secrets Act, under which the Board operated, specifically recognised the need for confidentiality and imposed penalties of up to two years imprisonment for anybody in the Board disclosing information. It then quoted my statement in full in which I stated:-

"It is indeed true I passed information to persons outside the Board. But I would stress that I had what were, in my opinion, perfectly valid reasons for so doing.

For some months as a member of the Board I had been alarmed by what I observed. It is my firm belief that all is not well in the use being made of public funds.

Thus, in 1966, without making any accusations, I offered the information I had to an MP for submission to Mr Ross, Secretary of State for Scotland.

When nothing had happened by early February, I considered the situation demanded early action. Further, I believed that people had a democratic right to a say in their own future, which appeared to be planned away on a very large scale unknown to them.

Having tried the correct authority without success, I then decided to act on my own. There seemed only one course open to me. I approached the Times"

My dismissal hit the headlines in the Scottish press. Amongst them were "SACKED", "Official Secrets Act threat to farmer", "This man leaked secrets", "The shame of Phil Durham", and, from the persistent James Laing of the *Daily Mail,* "These are the facts behind the Durham Affair". At the hastily called Sunday press conference in Inverness John Robertson claimed "on Friday night it became clear Mr Durham had persuaded the *Sunday Express* to run an article on him". He added that the allegations made were just a slanderous and completely unjustified attack on one man; there must have been a small group who put him up to it for certain reasons.

Such allegations were deeply disturbing to an unimaginative retired naval officer who had been trained from the age of thirteen at the Royal Naval College, Dartmouth to a life of discipline, honour, loyalty and responsibility and now found himself accused of dishonest, disloyal and irresponsible behaviour. It soon became obvious from the clicks and fading on our telephone that it was being tapped. Whatever damage to national security was I likely to cause?

Having left home early to attend the regular two-monthly meeting of the Highland Railway Users' Council, it was not till my return home that I discovered a press car parked at the farm road entrance to monitor comings and goings to Scotsburn. Meantime Reay Clarke as Chairman of the Easter Ross Land Use Committee had issued a statement repeating that they did not oppose industrial development but did insist it should be sited off the best agricultural land: he threatened to sue the Board for slander over their claim a small group had put me up to it. Professor Grieve back from Edinburgh issued a challenge to me to come out in the open with my allegations, To this, I replied "the thing I was trying to do was to get matters which I thought wrong put right without any public fuss. It seemed I had failed; now that this has come out into the open I am content to allow higher authorities to make the correct decision and investigate."

Alasdair Mackenzie, Ross & Cromarty MP, was quoted as saying he planned to call and see me on his return from Westminster later in the week, while Robert Maclennan agreed that he had raised my concerns last year with the Minister of State for Scotland and received an assurance that satisfied him that the Board was not acting contrary to the Act which set it up. When Magnus Magnusson from *The Scotsman* rang up, Jane told him to get lost. However he later discovered that cousins were staying in the Carlton Hotel close to the *Scotsman* office where he worked and they eventually agreed to accompany him across the road to a room where a table was deeply spread with information on Frank Thomson and his business dealings. In the small hours when they left the *Scotsman* office they agreed to suggest to us that we ought to talk to them.

I spent much of Wednesday drawing up and typing an account of the work I was doing in HIDB's employ, emphasising my interest and wish I had been able to continue to do it. Quite unnecessarily worried that my typewriter might be examined as evidence in some future legal action against me, I swapped with a friend. At lunchtime Reay Clarke rang in fury to say that John Robertson had just called on John Mann, Inverbreakie Farm, to tell him that the Board wished to buy his farm. As this had broken a promise that future plans for the land would first be discussed with the land use committee, it appeared that Robertson had panicked, HIDB having neither the authority nor the funds to make such an offer. In the afternoon, he had replied in answer to a question by Sir Kenneth Murray, a local land owner, solicitor and county councillor, that, given a 20% return on capital, it was quite plain to him there would be ample financial support from the most reputable financial sources of the very highest standard.

Charles Graham, editor of the *Scottish Daily Express,* made a long phone call asking me to publish in his paper my information which, while I did not agree to his suggestion, did make clear how well informed he was; because of this I did agree to keep in touch. Willie Munro, who had been a Vigilante trustee, rang to warn me that he had heard that Murdo Nicholson planned to visit me. Then, as it got dark, up the back stairs arrived Magnus Magnusson and David Kemp from the *Scotsman* Close-up team; they had made a series of visits, including the afternoon County Council meeting where the planning committee discussed the zoning of Inverbreakie Farm for industrial use, before arriving at Scotsburn for supper. We talked into the small hours as they prepared an article on Frank Thomson's business dealings. That day, Sybil Paterson had met Lady Maud Bailie in Inverness to discuss the situation. Somehow already Gordon Campbell, Tony Stoddart and Jean Harvey Anderson had seen a copy of my memorandum, to which her comment was "crikey".

It really did seem my attempts to avoid making my memorandum available had been in vain: so much for my ideas on confidentiality and getting everything cleared up without publicity. Apart from Ian Grimble, Robert Maclennan and Scottish Office ministers and, later, *The Times* I had shown it to nobody, and naively believed it would go no farther. What had started as a battle to avoid the misuse of public funds had become, perhaps inevitably, a campaign to get rid of Frank Thomson and maybe also John Robertson, who might seem to have become too closely linked with him and Occidental.

Chapter Seven
Politicians and Press take over.

OUR MP was the somewhat unlikely but very popular Alasdair Mackenzie, a Highland crofter born and bred who thought in his native Gaelic tongue, which resulted in an apparent hesitancy of speech while he translated into English. When he called, I felt free to allow him to read my memorandum before discussing my anxieties and failure to persuade Willie Ross to take action on it. Together we worked out two questions he might ask the Secretary of State in the House later in the week, and he agreed to my suggestion he should meet Hugh Fraser. Soon after he left, a retired naval officer friend, Captain Chubs Ranald, arrived accompanied by the County Convener who, when discussing the threats to prosecute me under the Official Secrets Act, suggested as it was me who had indirectly warned the Secretary of State and no-one else, claiming justification for passing on confidential information, any attack on my character must fail. Remembering Munro's earlier warning, I was careful in what I told him.

At the meeting of Inverness County Council that day, Lovat and several other councillors attacked the Board for secrecy and neglect of Highlanders' true interests, while others equally vehemently supported it.

The Friday HIDB meeting was attended by Dr Dickson Mabon, Minister of State, who denied that either he or his predecessor had received my information but did state that I was not to be prosecuted for my unfortunate misbehaviour. After the meeting Frank Thomson issued a statement that "I have stepped out from any situation whereby I could be accused of having a direct or indirect pecuniary interest in the Invergordon situation."

A visit from a cousin of Jane's who worked in Foreign Office intelligence commented that he considered that the amateurs had acquitted themselves creditably, accepting that the considerable use made of the almost certainly bugged phone was excusable in a rural area. He put us in touch with Mark Arnold Foster, a colleague of his, son in law of Naomi Mitcheson and a *Guardian* leader writer.

In next day's *Sunday Express* John Gordon followed up his previous week's Current Affairs article which had provoked the furore with further questions about HIDB and Frank Thomson. After enjoying a quiet lunch with Jane's parents at Ord, I received a call from David Kemp of *The Scotsman*. He read me an article due to appear the following day about the likely necessary expenditure of £10m on a new port at Invergordon should the petro-chemical plan proceed. Clearly the argument continued. As the *Scotsman* leader put it: "Mr Durham may have been ill advised in the way he went about it, but his concern at the way the Board has been conducting the Invergordon enterprise was only a reflection of a much larger public concern that was being voiced throughout the Highlands." That forenoon Alasdair rang to confirm he was to see Dickson Mabon next day.

At the meeting of the Land Use Committee that afternoon, members were told that Huntings Surveys in co-operation with the Macaulay Institute in Aberdeen were to tender for carrying out a land-use survey. One member, Ian Macpherson, Delny, due to his election as Chairman of the County Council's Planning Committee, offered to resign but was persuaded to remain. It was agreed that a request to carry out trial borings on Ord and Balintraid farms would be handled by solicitors, imposing terms for access, compensation and copies of the boring reports being made available to the farmers concerned. In reply to John Robertson's request that John Mann indicate at what price he would be prepared to sell Inverbreakie Farm it was agreed he should say £1,000 an acre but be free to negotiate any terms direct as long as he kept the Chairman informed. The support of the Agricultural Executive Committee was sought in any proposal to zone quality arable land for industrial use.

A bold centre page article appeared in the *Express* headed 'The Dissenter Invergordon' and quoting the views of Sir John Brooke, who had earlier resigned from the Vigilantes when they widened their remit beyond opposing rail closures. He attacked the economic viability, suitability, and employment prospects of the proposed petro-chemical complex.

In the evening Jane and I went to a drinks party given by Captain Chubs Ranald to offer support for my actions and attended by half a dozen retired naval officers and their wives, including the Lord Lieutenant, Captain Alec Matheson. When we were there the phone rang. From another room I answered Charles Graham from the *Scottish Daily Express* who proposed to drive up from Glasgow early the following morning and hoped we would see him: I agreed. My reputation placed on the line appeared to be surviving the attacks made on it: The Secretary of State had yet to face answering questions in the House from our M.P., from Jamie Davidson, Liberal M.P. for West Aberdeenshire who had rung me up to ask what was going on, and from Gordon Campbell, the shadow Minister of State for Scotland. I had moved from centre stage into the wings, or perhaps as prompter. After a stressful ten days this was a relief. Let others investigate HIDB's connections with Invergordon Chemical Enterprises and Occidental Oil which had caused me such concern. *The Scotsman* quoted Tony Stoddart, Opposition spokesman for agricultural affairs, supporting Easter Ross farmers in their criticism of the proposed destruction of high quality arable land for the sake of of a possible foreign-owned complex.

What I found so surprising next forenoon when Charles Graham called was that his interest lay in John Robertson and not Frank Thomson: why? He wanted to know about reported recent sackings of farm staff and questioned his connections with Alcan Aluminium which might follow Occidental Oil in taking advantage in supplies of cheap electricity. Only after discovering I could offer no help on this, did he start on the involvement between HIDB and Invergordon Chemical Enterprises. He planned to attend the public meeting to be held in the Invergordon Playhouse cinema that evening, at which I was later told a *Sunday Times* reporter claimed that everyone knew that John Robertson had effectively written the *Sunday Times* article which praised the petro-chemical plan. At this meeting the County Convener firmly refused to answer and indeed firmly stamped on questions seeking details of progress on possible future industrial development in Invergordon, the main reason for the calling of the meeting. Later that evening Charles Graham phoned to report that a *'Sunday Times* man' staying in the Royal Hotel had passed round to assembled press reporters photocopies of my memorandum. He also reported the resignation from the Board's employment of Tony Miller. to which I replied that I had heard of this before I was given notice and I did not consider this of any relevance. It was not till next afternoon, when I was told that Miller had made a statement supporting me and admitting that the Grants and Loans section had been concerned about loans to Thomson, that I had to say I hardly knew him; however I did agree to try and get hold of him for Graham. As I awaited a visit from a friend. Sandy Lawson, who was bringing Tony Stoddart, Tory agriculture spokesman, to Scotsburn, Jane set out to Delny Farm Cottages where Miller lived to try and collect him. On her return with him, Stoddart was here while he was questioned on the phone by the *Scottish Daily Express* which next day reported why he had left; as he had been a typical Board appointment of someone from outwith the Region and newly returned from South Africa rather than a native Highlander, I did not believe his contribution much help, while grateful to receive his support. However, at long last, Colin Simpson, his enchanting mini-skirted wife, and another journalist from the *Sunday Times* Insight team arrived just after supper, a mere six weeks after I had first approached Antony Vice, unaware he had newly left them to join *The Times*. When I discovered what they had planned for the centre page of the following Sunday's paper, the delay seemed well worth while. They had been appalled by the County Council meeting and said they had tried to stir things up a little. It was only after Magnus and David phoned to allow me to correct any inaccuracy in an article which was due to appear in next morning's paper that I realised that the *Scotsman* was about to scoop them. Clearly my work in awakening concern was done, and we could relax content that others would investigate. Meanwhile Charles Graham had been busy visiting Reay Clarke, Sybil Paterson and others. We awaited Friday, 17th March's press with keen anticipation.

The *Scotsman* 'Close Up' article stretched across both centre pages. Headed 'The business world of Frank Thomson', it contained much unknown to us and demanded the Secretary of State reply to Gordon Campbell's questions on the business interests of Highland Board members. Meanwhile in the *Express* Charles Graham under the headline 'What is going on?' began: "This green and once pleasant land is rent with rumour, riven by suspicion, divided by loyalties, now suffering the strain of stretching in several directions at once." He also demanded answers from Mr Ross.

In the afternoon, the Easter Ross Land Use Committee gave interested County Council members a conducted tour of the farms behind Invergordon likely to be destroyed by industrial development. Russell Johnson, Liberal M.P. for Inverness, rang up to ask to meet us and was invited to tea next day. He had been reported to claim that "in the row there was more smoke than fire, but there was a hell of a lot of smoke". He had continued that the sooner we found out how big the fire was the better. When he arrived with his fiancée, he accused me of faking Thomson's hotel bill, of falsifying expense claims from the Board and of trying to destroy it. He seemed surprised when shown the bill duly signed, and stamped for approved payment. So much for the Board's endeavours to blacken my character when he had called on them. This was not the only attempt being made to discredit me: the one I really resented was a demand made to examine Admiralty records of my naval career in the hope something discreditable lay within, of which I was informed by a friend working there.

The *Express* was at that time a broadsheet, long before it changed into a tabloid, and this allowed bold blocks of large headlines. When Graham next rang Scotsburn, I was out and Jane replied, suggesting to him that he must surely be getting fed up with the story, only to provoke the reaction: "Mrs Durham, this story is rather like Peyton Place: it can be continued almost indefinitely." When I returned home, he gave me details of the 26 separate questions for Mr Ross to answer which were to appear under the headline 'Where has all the cash gone in the Highland Fling? – some pertinent questions for Mr Ross.' They were all based on the information which I had included in my memorandum (see Appendix). By the time this article appeared, Mr Ross had stated that £38,187 had been awarded by HIDB to concerns in which Board members had a financial interest.

The 19th March *Sunday Times* article across the centre page was headlined 'How the Highland Board was railroaded'. It included a map of the area and a copy of a statement in a report that an option had been secured on 1,200 acres of land behind Invergordon, a fact totally denied by the land owners involved. The article followed Frank Thomson's career from small chartered accountant's business through Invergordon Distillery to the Scottish Vigilantes' campaign against Beeching rail closures and on to Polyscot Companies and Invergordon Chemical Enterprises' endeavour to foster a petro chemical complex from its offices in Kincraig House, part owned by him as a member of a farmers' consortium. The article concluded with Professor Grieve's refusal to be interviewed by the Insight team unless they gave an assurance that the subject of the Invergordon project and Mr Thomson's business interests would not be brought into the discussion.

By Monday, 20th March pressure on the Secretary of State was mounting fast. He had had time to consider a memorandum from Sir Matthew Campbell noting a meeting he had held in the Board's office with Frank Thomson about his position in relation to the proposed petro chemical complex. Thomson had refused to rule out his accepting a directorship but did agree to take neither shares nor debentures in the venture, making the suggestion that a new company replacing Invergordon Chemical Enterprises could form the vehicle for the new development. He had added that, should he eventually have to decide between remaining on the Board or accepting a directorship of the company, he would weigh up how best he could help the Highlands. Sir Matthew, in a postscript, pointed out that Thomson had been less than candid over his continuing membership of the Kincraig partnership.

Scots Tory M.P.s had already announced they were to meet that day in Westminster to decide what steps to take over the HIDB, after hearing the report of Tony Stoddart on his fact-finding trip to the North, where he had met farmers from Easter Ross 'including Philip Durham and Reay Clarke.' He had also noted the declaration of interest made by John Robertson over a loan of £7,500 to RTS Potatoes who rented from him the Admiralty built mine filling station at Nigg used for the treatment of seed potatoes, the rent of which had then risen from £350 to £1,000 a year. From this meeting was to come the motion tabled next day "That this House deplores the refusal of the Secretary of State for Scotland to give information about the Highlands and Islands Development Board for which he was asked and calls upon the Secretary of State to make a statement in the House before the Easter recess in order to allay rumour, innuendo and speculation which can only be damaging to the reputation of the Board". This motion was signed in the names of Michael Noble (Argyll), Antony Stoddart (West Edinburgh), Gordon Campbell (Moray & Nairn), Ian MacArthur (Perth & East Stirlingshire), Norman Wyllie, Q.C. (Edinburgh Pentlands), and Hector Munro (Dumfries). Decisions could no longer be postponed.

Emerging from an all-day meeting of the Board in Inverness an angry Frank Thomson read to waiting press reporters a four page statement which gave details of the Polyscot companies, of the £25,000 received from HIDB in July, the £300 tendering grant for hotel plans, and the application made by Ross-shire Engineering controlled by Polyscot in November for a further £25,000. The statement made no reference to Invergordon Chemical Enterprises.

With the answer to the Tory opposition motion due on Thursday, Willie Ross could delay no longer; Grieve, Robertson and Thomson were summoned to the House of Commons at 7 p.m. on Tuesday to meet himself, the Minister of State and Sir Matthew Campbell.

"The Secretary of State opened the meeting to state it was essential that, in his statement, he should give as much information as possible to avoid putting himself in the position of having further information extracted from him bit by bit. The situation was very serious in the eyes of both the House and of the Government and his own future might well be involved in it. What was concerning the public was that a member of the Board appeared to have a very big stake in the success of the projected petro chemical complex.

"Mr Thomson referred to the agreement between Occidental Petroleum and Invergordon Chemical Enterprises which consisted, in effect, of himself and Mr Colin Campbell, backed by certain other interests. He admitted the agreement was undoubtedly very valuable to ICE and repeated earlier assurances given to Sir Matthew Campbell, but accepted he had not considered how he would divest himself of his share of any profits. He further referred to his membership of the Kincraig partnership and the interest of

82

his family trust in Messrs Duffy, Travel Agents which had been used by the Board before the Trust took over. He said the recent publicity had been exceedingly damaging to his interests and that his associate in the Polyscot Enterprises, Mr Colin Campbell, was facing a serious financial situation. His legal advisers had advised that he sue *The Sunday Times* in respect of the article on him which appeared on 19th March.

"The Secretary of State said that sooner or later Mr Thomson would require to leave the Board. The timing of his departure was a matter of great difficulty: the present was a very embarrassing time for him to leave. In this connection he referred to the statement in the *Sunday Times* article that the Board had committed the Government and was given an assurance by Mr Thomson that neither he nor any other members of the Board present, nor the Board itself, had given any assurance committing the Government. The Secretary of State repeated that the whole project would have to be assessed by the Government on the basis of the investment required for docks, housing, power, etc. He referred to Mr John Robertson's letter to Sir Frank Schon which appeared to be a very serious commitment, and said the Board must not give promises which it could not itself fulfil. Mr Robertson admitted that his letter had been incautious and accepted the Secretary of State's censure and assured the Secretary of State that no similar letters had been issued.

"In summing up the Secretary of State said he would require to speak to the Prime Minister about the credibility of his statement on the objectivity of the Board's attitude. There was a strong likelihood that the public would see the position as one in which Mr Thomson was using his position on the Board to further his own interests. It had to be accepted that people could act in a perfectly fair and proper manner but nevertheless be misunderstood to an extent which compromised the position of the Board. It was clear that Mr Thomson was more essential to the petrochemical project than to the Board. Against this background the major difficulty lay in Mr Thomson's advocacy of the complex in two capacities."

It is remarkable that Professor Grieve appears to have remained silent throughout this meeting, seeming to give another clear indication of his inability to justify why the Board he chaired had placed the Scottish Secretary under such severe pressure, surely a total failure in leadership. Without any decision on possible resignations the trio were told to return to Dover House the following forenoon.

That evening Mark Arnold Foster from *The Guardian* rang to discuss at length regional boards, the future of which seemed to him of great importance. I suggested that their ability to take over and, if necessary overrule, the responsibilities of officials appointed by democratically elected local authorities had caused concern in the Highlands. Later resignations were to confirm this. Hardly had I put down the phone when it again rang. Paul Foot from *Private Eye* wanted to question me about my sacking. I answered warily, not having appreciated the magazine's political influence. This was to lead to his devoting his whole Footnotes article to my and the *Times's* actions.

The article ended:- "Information that Durham had sent documents to *The Times* could only have come originally from the *Times* itself. So if you happen to have any worries about your employers which you want investigated or publicised be sure to send it to the new, dynamic, crusading *Times,* preferably to the new, dynamic, crusading Business Section.

If you do that, you can be sure of two things:

(1) The information will be totally ignored and the exact opposite will be published

(2) You will shortly lose your job."

The *Guardian* article, when it appeared, contained the suggestion that "Mr Durham's document appeared so expertly assembled that it suggested skilled activity, possibly beyond the range of Easter Ross farmers concerned about the public weal." The repeated suggestion that I was acting as a mouthpiece of the lairds, or the farmers, or the Tories I found mildly insulting.

Chapter Eight
Resignation and its aftermath

IT IS UNCLEAR quite what went on in Dover House the day before the Secretary of State was to make his statement but, among the Government papers released under the 30-year rule (SEP12/560), is a memorandum sent to the Prime Minister and separately to his Private Secretary which began:– "Following our brief discussion today, I have seen Mr Frank Thomson of the Highlands and Islands Development Board and he has agreed to resign. I enclose a copy of the statement which I propose to make tomorrow. I have done my best to restrict its length but the subject has many facets."

After listing the assistance given to businesses in which members of the Board had declared an interest, the statement continued to state that, while the proposed petrochemical and associated development in the Invergordon area could be a highly desirable project, a great deal of study and investigation would be required before its feasibility could be established. It must therefore be made clear there had not been, nor could there be at present, any commitment by the Government in this matter.

The statement continued to consider Mr Frank Thomson's position. It made clear that, as Chairman of Invergordon Chemical Enterprises, he had an interest in the petrochemical development should it go ahead, but would take steps to see that he did not derive any profit from either this or his membership of the Kincraig Partnership. However, Mr Thomson was not able to assure Mr Ross that he would not accept an appointment in the enterprise should it eventuate. In all the circumstances he had decided that in order to avoid any possible misunderstanding he should now resign from the Board and the Secretary of State had accepted his resignation. He did so with regret knowing as he did the enthusiasm, concern and effort he had put into the development of the Highlands.

The Scotsman reported that Professor Grieve watched from a public gallery as Mr Ross made the most difficult statement of his public life. Sometimes the Secretary of State's voice faltered with emotion, sometimes he stumbled over words as he read from his carefully prepared brief. In the course of the debate which followed, Donald Dewar pleaded for an end to this stupid and needless witch hunt against Mr Thomson, who had now been cleared by investigation. I was accused of disloyalty to the Board and, when I was informed of this, I issued a press statement as follows:-

"I am far from jubilant over the latest developments – in fact I am very sad that this should have happened to the Highland Board in which so many people had placed their hopes for the future.

"I am saddened to learn that I am accused of disloyalty to the Highland Board. My only care was that the interests of the Highlands should not be betrayed by the Board. I have lived and worked in the Highlands for 20 years and was a very junior employee of this new board who felt that there was something that must be investigated as I was unhappy at what I saw going on.

"My most compelling loyalty is to the Highlands. Had I kept silent it might have been the Highland people who suffered in ignorance of decisions until it was too late. I am willing to abide by their judgement. All I sought was an investigation. It appears to me that this investigation has now begun, and I am happy to leave it to other people in Parliament to take what action is necessary. I am

very sad that we have come to this pass as I believe that what has happened has been detrimental both to the Highlands and the Board."

As Frank Thomson set off for a holiday with his family to Majorca he issued a farewell statement and it only seems fair to reproduce it in full:-

"'Whither goest thou?' might well be the question posed to me at this moment. Nobody can ever hope to foresee what the future holds. But I am sure of one thing – that, so long as the Highlands and Islands have men of the integrity and compassion, initiative and vision of Bob Grieve and the other members of the Highland Board we will be served well.

"They will have my whole-hearted support. If any persons think that I leave the Board lightly, then they do not know me and cannot begin to understand the grief in my heart. Or, if they think for one moment that they can continue the vile campaign against the Board or any of its members, I am now free to take positive action. And I am confident I shall be backed by the overwhelming majority of the people in the Highlands, so many of whom, despite the recent campaign, have already indicated their confidence in and support for the Board. We who truly love the Highlands have lived through a dark period of anguish, despair and misery these last few weeks. We must set aside these feelings and, all of us, Gaelic and English speaking, bind ourselves together in a united force to make the Highlands the place we want it to be – where our children can live in social significance and economic parity with those who live in other parts of Britain.

"When we can agree to disagree objectively, when we can trust our fellow men, when we can begin to understand the personal sacrifices of those in public office – only then will we breed the leaders we need so desperately in the Highlands of Scotland."

John Gordon's article on 5th March had led to the last eighteen day's publicity which it had taken to achieve the investigation and correction of what I believed was wrong. Press focus had gradually transferred from a waiting car-load of journalists at the pillars at the bottom of our road to observe comings and goings at Scotsburn to their later siege of the HIDB office in Inverness.

I could not but feel some sympathy for Board members, in particular Thomson and Robertson who were watching the premature and unwelcome unveiling of their brainchild; indeed, John consulted William Munro for guidance, saying he was at his wits' end, only to be advised to lie low, do nothing and say as little as possible till the storm blew over. Our one regret was that, out of the limelight, Colin Campbell and his family might face near insolvency from the likely collapse of the house of cards piled with the Polyscot group of companies on top. Now, at least there was time to acknowledge the letters, many from strangers, that had been arriving with each daily post in support of my action. Surprisingly, for the local community was deeply divided over the petro-chemical plan, only one anonymous, illiterate letter from Stornoway was written in condemnation, likening me to Patrick Sellar. Two letters in particular brought me real pleasure. Alec Dickson from Community Service Volunteers, whom I had met when working on my youth activity survey for the Board, wrote:

"I am writing very briefly – and very personally – to express my very sincere sympathy at the extra-ordinarily shabby and disgraceful treatment meted out to you.

"I would like you to know how deeply I admire the stand that you have taken in regard to basic integrity in public affairs. How very cheering it is to discover that there are still 'Village Hampdens' in Britain today who will not condone bureaucratic injustice.

"It does not always happen that those who stand out against injustice and have the satisfaction of seeing their stand publicly vindicated, are necessarily reinstated or acknowledged. But, I do hope that your attitude is eventually rewarded.

"Whatever happens to you now, and wherever you may be, I

do wish you all good luck, and salute what you have done."

Then Naomi Mitchison a little later wrote:- *"I read most of the stuff which came out in the papers and the various whitewashings in press cuttings when I was away in Africa. As far as I can make out, you are the one person who has behaved as I would myself."* That really pleased me.

There were many in Ross-shire who were convinced that heavy industry, despite its possible pollution and other disadvantages, was the much needed catalyst for the regeneration of the Highlands, and deeply regretted the set-back to such a development my action had involved. My father-in-law was castigated in a shop by Mrs Rhind, a local councillor and shopkeeper, for selfishly standing in the way of Highland development. The county clerk, James Dunlop, though more discreet, was another supporter, perhaps from a realisation of the high rateable value to county finances a petro-chemical complex would create. These rifts would continue and even deepen over a decade with the rise and fall of the British Aluminium smelter.

During the week following the announcement of Thomson's resignation, Lovat and Hugh Fraser visited us to consider a forthcoming Lords debate. At it Atholl was to raise the facts behind the *Times* article, Cromartie, with whom I had kept in touch, secrecy and the rumour that Occidental Oil had promised directorships to both Thomson and Robertson; while Lovat would seek the replacement of Grieve by Joe Grimond as a national figure in whom Highlanders would have confidence. Later I fielded an interminable phone call from Burton keen to join in; he referred to Michael Noble's recent demand for a statement on the connections between ICE, Occidental Oil and HIDB.

Ian Grimble, as Chairman of Caithness and Sutherland Labour constituency party, attended the Annual Conference of the Scottish Labour Party in Dundee and caused a stir by going to the rostrum and saying about the Highland Board :– "I think it would be ungrateful of the Labour Party in Scotland today if we didn't thank the Press for what they have done in the last fortnight to brief us on the subject, particularly the *Scottish Daily Express* and that distinguished native of Dundee, John Gordon of the *Sunday Express*. I gave Mr Ross as much information as I could at Brighton in October when I was the only delegate from the seven crofter counties."

He continued: "The chimpanzee's tea party at the Highland Development Board is over. I hope there is nothing left for us to do about that except pick up the banana skins. Now is the time for the Board to get on with the task it was set up to perform – and that is the reclamation of the immense man-made wilderness that covers half the land area of Scotland."

On the last day of the three-day Labour Party Conference Robert Maclennan spoke just before the Secretary of State and claimed that what he had passed on to him in Brighton had been given him by a constituent. He claimed "I happened to be present at the rather short encounter when the mention of the Board's priorities was discussed and, at that very short encounter which lasted only about three minutes, not one word was said about the disquiet which finally led to a resignation from the Board." This statement let the Secretary of State off the hook but later, after a stormy meeting with his agent in Thurso, Maclennan was forced to retract, and publicly apologise to Ian Grimble, admitting that the meeting had lasted longer than three minutes and, indeed, he had not been present all the time; Ian accepted this apology, but the damage had been done.

John Gordon's Current Affairs column on the Sunday bowed out of the row, referring to claims of the need for a Press Ombudsman and suggesting that people would get justice in any fight with bureaucracy far less effectively from any ombudsman than from a fair newspaper "which, as recent odd happenings in the affairs of the Highland Development Board showed so startlingly, isn't the *Times.*"

On the morning of the House of Lords debate Scottish press

headlines were devoted to an assessment by Hugh Fraser of the financial and practical implications of the petro-chemical plan. He summarised the falling world price and over-production of urea and fertilisers and questioned HIDB's claim to be able to produce electricity at a cost of only a third of a penny a unit, well below even the most optimistic forecast for either atomic or gas turbine generation. His brother's call in the Lords for the replacement of Grieve by a national figure such as Joe Grimond, M.P. for Orkney and Shetland, was widely reported next day, on the evening of which Chubs Ranald rang us up to ask whether Mr Colin Taylor, Ross and Cromarty County Planning Officer and his wife could come over to discuss his intended resignation at the morrow's planning committee meeting. He brought with him a statement he intended to issue. It seemed that he and his assistant planning officer, with two members of staff, were all to announce their resignation the following day. At his request we rang *The Scotsman* and, after he had spoken to Ian Mackay, an assistant editor, it was agreed that he would write an article for them. His complaint was his exclusion from involvement in the secret plans being made by Board staff which placed him in an impossible position to advise his council employers. With essential details suppressed, he was being encouraged to support in principle applications from firms likely to be involved in the petro-chemical plan. He found himself in an impossible situation. At the March meeting of the Planning Committee his reports and recommendations were repeatedly ignored or rejected and, indeed at one point, he had been told to "sit down and shut up". Others appeared to be in possession of information denied him. His position had become untenable. Consultants had been appointed by the Board to plan a linear city but he had been neither involved nor consulted. Planning was a public process and its administration was similarly a matter for general knowledge. Negotiations behind closed doors could only bring it into disrepute.

In his article on the *Scotsman's* centre page on Saturday, 8th

April, Taylor wrote that he believed the real fault in the Highland situation seemed to be in the Board being established as a "development" but not as a "planning" authority. Development could never be divorced from planning because town and country planning was basically the control of development. Any one of the planning authorities in the Moray Firth Growth Area (there were five) could choose to ignore the plans produced by the Board at great expense by their own team of experts. This article emphasised the dilemma which the establishment of such unelected Government sponsored bodies posed, as indeed I had suggested to the *Guardian's* leader writer earlier.

Our peaceful Sunday was disrupted when, in the afternoon, a car drew up on the gravel. Two young men emerged and announced they were from the *Times* and would like to ask me some questions. Keeping them standing there I told them I thought it a nerve for the *Times* to approach me after its disgraceful behaviour, and brought to their attention the *Private Eye* article about its betrayal. When they replied that they did not read this magazine I told them to wait till I found my copy and then read them Paul Foot's "Hard times in the Highlands" piece. They appeared uneasy and impatient, claiming that *Private Eye* was a scandalous and untrue rag. Jane, who had been feeding the baby, having heard the conversation thought I had been too nasty and invited them to have tea with us.

During tea I inquired over the health of Roy Mackie, only to be told they did not know him and, when I expressed surprise at their having neglected this obvious source of information, was told that they worked for the *Times* news team which was completely separate from the Business Section. Then, as we had guests coming for drinks, I perhaps unwisely invited the two reporters to return after supper

On their return I explained the work I was doing in the Board, my interest in it and why I wished it to be successful. At this point Sybil Paterson, whom we had invited to come and act as an independent witness to what transpired, arrived in time to hear me indicate to our visitors some of the more obvious untruths and half truths in the article which the *Times* had published on 25th February. This seemed to make our guests impatient and one of them announced that this was not helping them at all. When I inquired whether they had come to discover facts or, if not, why they had come to disturb our Sunday, I was told they had come to question me.

In particular, I found the hook-nosed Garry Lloyd, who did most of the questioning, one of the most unpleasant characters I had ever had the misfortune to meet. His manner was hectoring and sometimes downright rude, he failed to listen to my answers to his questions and constantly interrupted. It became more and more clear he was determined to force me to admit I was opposed to industry, brushing aside my telling him of my involvement in the writing of 'Highland Opportunity' two years earlier. Next he mentioned papers being pushed under Strathclyde's Inverness hotel bedroom door at dead of night and said he knew who had done this, causing mirth and ironic laughter when he replied to my question on the source of this information that journalists never reveal their sources. Sibyl Paterson who had arranged the delivery of the memorandum particularly enjoyed this.

From constant questions about Ian Grimble, Robert Maclennan and the Minister of State it became more and more clear their remit was to prove John Robertson could have acquired a copy of my memorandum from a source other than the *Times*. Eventually from the same question over and over again I lost my temper and Jane told our visitors they were abusing our hospitality and had better go. They made no move to leave and repeated once again that I should admit that I was part of a plot to destroy the Highland Board.

Eventually Jane said 'You must now leave as I am becoming hysterical at your behaviour and I still have half an hour's baby food to prepare before I go to bed. Still they made no move, so I wheeled my chair out of the room and was followed into the hall by

Lloyd still arguing even as I opened the front door; as they unwillingly left, I asked them to behave reasonably for they had been treated with great good manners despite the provocation they had given. After getting into their car they continued talking together with no attempt to start the engine, leaving me at the open door in the cold night air waiting to see them off. At long last they did leave.

When, in the course of the last month, we had dealt with over a score of pressmen, this was the first and only time we had suffered this type of discourtesy, of arrogant and repetitive questioning and of unwillingness to leave when asked so to do. The three of us subsided and discussed the visit and our visitors: at the time the US was suffering from the extremes of McCarthyism, whose two most notorious practitioners of the art of exerting extreme pressure on those suspected of communist leanings and connections were named Cohn and Schine, and so Garry Lloyd and Dan van der Vat were renamed and five days later their five column centre page article below photographs of Michael Noble, myself and Frank Thomson appeared in the *Times*. It was headed: *Cloak and dagger in Macbeth country. International intrigue grips the Highlands (and Islands)* and continued "The Highlands are gripped by an atmosphere of intrigue which has all the classical elements of John Buchan. They included stolen papers, alleged telephone tapping, character assassination, veiled threats, secret meetings, palpitations of international business interests and an extraordinary tale of a raid by a wartime hero, said to have sneaked down an hotel corridor at dead of night to thrust illicit documents under the bedroom door of a sleeping baron.

"The furore threatens not only the Highland Board's very existence, and the new industrial complex, but, increasingly, also the career of Mr William Ross, Secretary of State for Scotland who has powerful and determined enemies.

"For this reason Highlanders with purely parochial objections to the Board have become unlikely bedfellows of sophisticated entrepreneurs out to smash a potentially formidable rival to long established concerns."

The article then quoted a long interview with Frank Thomson which followed his past activities, his break up with Max Rayne, and the idea that the complex would be the catalyst for electricity dependent industries justifying a linear city of 250,000 inhabitants. It continued by mentioning Ian Grimble and Robert Maclennan warning the Secretary of State and, after no result, my sending my memorandum to the *Times*. I was quoted, after my sacking, as knowing the risks I was taking and of commenting "I did what I believed to be my duty, and have no regrets". The article then concluded by reporting a meeting in 1965 between Dr Beeching, deputy chairman of ICI, Max Rayne and Thomson representing ICE. Beeching was quoted as saying "we thought people who were ignorant about this might get themselves into trouble and, incidentally, get us into trouble as well. All we proposed was that we should give them our assessment of the situation. Following this meeting ICI heard no more about it from either Mr Rayne or Mr Thomson."

A few days later the *Times* published a letter from Lord Dundee criticising the unhelpful article which claimed to list the implications of the proposed complex, and concluded: "*as for the Highlanders we are told that they have 'so far shown little awareness of these implications, though an idea being mooted in the area should have given them a glaring clue.' This last statement at least seems credible, for the Highlanders, whether they share their beds with sophisticated entrepreneurs or not, are mainly sensible folk who are not tremendously interested in listening to drivel. Your article which is subheaded 'Cloak and dagger in Macbeth country' could indeed be well described by the passage about Macbeth's phantom dagger:-*

> *Art thou not, fatal vision, sensible*
> *To feeling as to sight? or art thou but*
> *A dagger of the mind, a false creation*
> *Proceeding from the heat oppressed brain. –*

or *should we say proceeding from the chain reaction to the complex?"*

After that, *The Times* kept its silence, but *The Scotsman* printed a similar sized article by Reay Clarke headed "A five stage plan for the Highlands". In it he quoted Sir Frank Fraser Darling's preface to "West Highland Survey" published in 1954, describing the increasing decline in fertility and the impoverishment of the land. Clarke, in his suggestion how to build more fertile soil and reduce impoverishment of the land, suggested a long term way ahead in five stages: first, a land capability survey by geographers and ecologists, not by farming or forestry interests; next, its assessment; then identify a valley or island and involve local people in the preparation of a development plan; fourth, act on the plan, with continuing assessment of its results; and, finally, after evaluation and any necessary modification, repeat it elsewhere.

He believed that, by the soil becoming more fertile and the countryside more beautiful, the human problems would be easier to deal with, and suggested the whole five stage plan would cost less than the sums being spent on feasibility studies to bring heavy industry to the Highlands.

Chapter Nine
No petro-chemical announcement

I HAD neither heard anything from nor had any contact with John Rollo since 17th February, 1967 and now, 30 years later, learn about him and John Robertson from a newly released memorandum, marked <u>Confidential</u> from Sir Matthew Campbell:-

He wrote: "Secretary, This is to put on record what I told you on the telephone about the conversation I had at the annual dinner of the Highland Fund on 11th April.

"<u>Professor Grieve</u> was taciturn and subdued and we did no more than exchange pleasant civilities.

"<u>Mr Rollo</u> was buoyant. When I asked if he and Professor Grieve had a talk with you that afternoon he said he had "but of course they were talking about things I knew nothing about at all". He had never been consulted; these things were never discussed at the Board. He went on to say that Professor Grieve had without any formal agreement by the Board promised the Jack Holmes group work for the next five years at a cost of at least £250,000 and possibly nearer £400,000. This was for MFD.

"The Jack Holmes Group were certainly under the impression that they were being engaged for this purpose and were taking on more staff. They had proposed that Messrs Huntings should carry out an aerial survey and re-draw the map of the area, but that he (Mr Rollo) had turned that down.

"Finally he said that he personally did not think that Ross-Shire Engineering Ltd was sound and that he would turn their application for further help down. He made some remarks about the financial genius who was behind that group.

"I found this combination of euphoria and irresponsibility alarming: but Mr Rollo is so buoyant that there can be no question, while he is in that mood, of suggesting to him that he might vacate the Deputy Chairmanship. I did not even hint at the possibility.

"Mr Fasken is deeply disturbed on two counts. First he says that the rift between the "civil Servants" and the "commercials" on the Board is almost impossible for him to cope with. He attributes this to the encouragement that the Chairman and Mr John Robertson have given to the view that the Board is not a Government Department and to their consistently disparaging remarks about civil servants, St Andrew's House, Government Departments *ad hoc genus omne*. He remarked wryly that in the recent hubbub Professor Grieve had said that there were not enough civil servants around. But this was only a passing phase.

"Mr John Robertson gives cause for more serious concern. Mr Fasken said he wanted to impress on us very clearly that Mr Robertson has learned no lessons at all from what the Secretary of State said to him on 22nd March. He had returned to Inverness in the greatest of good spirits and full of enthusiasm for the way the Secretary of State had spoken about the Board's proposals. However he has since then been deeply engaged with representatives of Alcan, and Mr Fasken does not know what had taken place, or the extent to which Mr Robertson had entered into commitments.

"Mr Fasken said that he wanted us to understand that it was Mr Robertson's deliberate policy, in affairs like this petro-chemical project, to push ahead, enter into commitments, get the job done, and tidy up the bits afterwards. He had been furious at being made to sign the "retracting" letters to the firms to whom he had promised cheap electricity and had put pressure on Mr Fasken to send a 'mind your own business' reply to Mr Russell's letter about Bechtel. When Mr Fasken refused he added a mock-offensive P.S. himself.

"Finally Mr Robertson has been making dark hints that an article would shortly appear in *The Times*. Mr Fasken does not think that Mr Robertson is inspiring this article: but Lord Strathclyde's message to Mr Hume seems confirmation that the *Times* is brewing something.

"Having in mind what Mr Rollo had told me about Jack Holmes I asked Mr Fasken if any arrangements had been entered into. He said no, but that Mr Spaven had been instructed to draw up draft terms of agreement, and that this draft would be coming before the Board. I gathered that meantime Jack Holmes has been engaged on a temporary basis.

"I then asked Mr Fasken if he was sure all payments actually made by the Board were properly authorised. He assured me that they were. I then asked Mr Fasken whether he should not have a full-time finance officer to assist him. After some doubts he agreed this would be useful; adding however that he would not wish to part entirely with Mr Mitchell, who had great possibilities as a projects officer. He said that he agreed with me that a strong Deputy Chairman was necessary, but he saw the difficulties.

"Finally, I had some veiled hints from Mr JCN Baillie. He confirmed that there would be an article in *The Times* – perhaps he adds nothing to what we have heard from Lord Strathclyde. He also said that Mr Thomson's affairs were in difficulty."

Willie Ross must have been appalled by both the genie which had emerged from the bottle and the possible impossibility of forcing it back in again before it destroyed him. Leaving aside John Rollo who had grave reservations, two of the three members he had appointed to the Board, including the Chairman, appeared to have been involved in an attempt to frog-march the Government into accepting a fait accompli, and remained in post, apparently

impervious to criticism. Further an unbridgeable chasm appeared
to divide Chairman and Deputy Chairman: no wonder the
Secretary was close to despair. Since Frank Thomson's resignation
and John Robertson's determination to press on with the petro-
chemical plan, Sir Matthew Campbell had required to travel up
from St Andrew's House to Inverness regularly to attend Board
plenary meetings to check on what went on. Some of the press,
supported by the Tories, were baying for his resignation, while
there seemed no chance of any voluntary Board retirements. The
predicament of the Sorcerers' Apprentice came forcibly to mind.
Soon he would have to face a Scottish Grand Committee debate.
Meantime he had requested Sir Douglas Haddow to receive Mr
Frank Thomson in Dover House.

At that meeting among the points brought to Sir Douglas's
attention there were:-

Mr Durham. Mr Thomson said that Mr Durham was a
continuing irritant in the Inverness and Ross-shire area. He was an
embittered man out to break the Board. He was enticing journalists
such as Messrs Magnusson and Kemp to carry out a press vendetta
against both the present members of the Board and Mr Thomson
himself. This was particularly hard to endure when all the targets of
the campaign lived and worked in the Inverness area. He went on
to suggest that action should be taken to have Mr Durham
prosecuted for theft. He himself did not propose to take any civil
action against him for, for example, libel. He said that as a result of
the campaign against him, his creditors were pursuing him, but
claimed not to be unduly worried by this, claiming recent press
reports had understated his assets and exaggerated his liabilities.

Sunday Times "Insight" article. Mr Thomson said he had
instructed a firm of London solicitors to institute libel proceedings
against *The Sunday Times*. He did not expect it would be contested
in the courts and expected an out-of-court settlement.

Vice Chairman of the HIDB. Mr Thomson said that the
conduct of Mr Rollo, both in the Board offices and outside, made it

very difficult for the Chairman and other members of the Board to operate efficiently. He felt that Mr Rollo's position on the Board would have to be reviewed.

General aspects of Moray Firth Development. Mr Thomson said the Government should be right behind the plans for the development of the petro-chemical complex at Invergordon and went on to list the commercial advantages of the plans. In response to a question from Sir Douglas, he agreed that cheap power was in no way essential for the petro-chemical complex, although of course it was vital for the aluminium and phosphorous proposals. He seemed disconcerted when Sir Douglas said that it should not be regarded as automatic that investment grants would be paid for the construction of a major power station by a private company or consortium at Invergordon. He emphasised that the establishment of a commercial operation at Invergordon on the scale envisaged would involve considerable demands on public expenditure to meet infrastructure requirements, for which a figure of £25m. would not be unrealistic, and it could not be assumed that such a sum would be available.

Early in May a drilling rig to bore a possible site for an atomic power station arrived to investigate land on Ord and Balintraid farms, revealing rock 65 feet below the surface. Meanwhile a promise given to supply vast quantities of electricity at well below any realistic price to an American fertiliser firm had the Minister of State, Dr Dickson Mabon, rushing north to Inverness to force its retraction by John Robertson, after a considerable row. Only because of a signed contract with too great a cost of cancellation did the trial borings proceed.

While the boring was in progress, Hunting's land capability survey arrived to confirm the remarkable quality of the land chosen for development. It showed that 2.3% of the land (all located on the two chosen farms) was of Class 1 horticultural land, while no less than 84.9% was Class 2 top quality arable land with a mere 12.8 % of lower quality but still cultivatable land. None of the land was of qualities 5 to 8.

On 26th May Willie Ross made the Secretary of State's first visit to HIDB's office in Inverness since he had set it up. At a press conference after the meeting he stated it was most unfortunate Easter Ross had got the impression decisions about the complex had been made because they had not. It was four days after this visit that the much delayed, rewritten first HIDB annual report was published. Referring only to the year up to December, 1966 it was spared reporting on events thereafter but did mention their formal submission to the Secretary of State on 28th December giving their ideas for urban/industrial development of the Moray Firth area and seeking support. It even devoted a paragraph to my studies on possible future promotion of youth activities in the region. Then the local paper featured an advertisement of the proposed zoning for industry of Inverbreakie and part of Ord farm, giving individuals six weeks to forward any representations.

The flames of petro-chemical controversy were rekindled by an article written by Mark Arnold Foster in the *Guardian* on 29th June. This reported that a decision on the proposal had been vetoed for two years. Despite a denial, Frank Thomson suggested this was an inspired leak and that Willie Ross would make some statement on a visit to Inverness planned a week later. The *Guardian* article stated "neither Mr Ross nor his officials are opposed to the Board's main plan, a linear city running round the head of the Moray Firth. What the Scottish Office has disapproved is the expenditure of what would be a very high proportion of the available public funds on this one project within the city plan".

Reaction to this article was not long delayed: it provoked a special HIDB meeting being called hours after John Robertson had publicly attacked St Andrew's House for a deliberate policy of muddle, frustration and confusion towards much of the Board's development plans, accusing Sir Douglas Haddow of being the main stumbling block. He threatened to resign should the *Guardian* report prove true and stated that, in that case, he believed Mr Ross also should resign, for he would have failed to back Highland, indeed Scottish development. HIDB had no statement to make after this meeting which John did not attend but instead flew south to St Andrew's House, white with rage and indignation. After this outburst, his early resignation appeared inevitable and, further, it was being suggested that George Thompson, MP for Dundee, would replace Willie Ross himself as Secretary of State.

When, the day before the Board meeting to be attended by Mr Ross, Mark Arnold Foster called at the HIDB office he was kept waiting till after the London papers arrived off the night train before Jimmy Grassie, the Board press officer would see him. He was unable to get any answer to his repeated question of the cost per job created of the proposed complex. He did however receive a hint that possibly Alcan rather than Occidental might be the chosen developer. When, in the evening, he met John Robertson he found him not then in a resigning mood, hoping still his point of view would reach acceptance. This was not to be and so it was that, next morning, he handed the Secretary of State the following very rational letter of resignation:-

"When you were good enough to invite me to join the Highlands and Islands Development Board I wrote to you outlining my views on how it must go. In particular I said that I firmly believe that big enterprise and a willingness to do things differently from heretofore were how to solve the problem. I added that my understanding of your intentions for the Board was such that you would not want anyone holding this view on it but that, if it was acceptable to you, I would be happy to serve.

"Since then I have been concerned among other things with big enterprise in connection with Moray Firth Development and I have been increasingly dismayed by the attitude of the Scottish Office. This has been communicated both to you and your senior officials.

"It has become clear from our work that the problem is quite soluble over all the area covering half of Scotland, given the will to solve it and willingness to deploy the necessary resources.

"I see no sign whatever of the requisite will to solve the problem on the part of the Scottish Office and of course in the terms of the Act that is crucial. The attitude to proposals of real substance is uniformly a negative search for the maximum of difficulty. To this is added a degree of indecision and confusion that is quite startling. The Board has emphasised that we do not stand in a static situation and that delay or indecision are just as effective in driving away any development as a straight no.

"Turning to Moray Firth Development and putting aside the 'petro-chemical complex' and the induced controversy surrounding it, the position is that you have before you two major submissions from the Board and definite major proposals from commercial interests of the very highest repute and standing made jointly to us and the Board of Trade. I say confidently that when these proposals can be made public it will be apparent to all that not only are they excellent for Highland development but also for the UK in general and the balance of payments in particular. Your reply contained only a peremptory instruction to do nothing whatever about them and to have no contact with the firms concerned.

"This is characteristic with all our contacts with your departments on major proposals which involve using methods novel to the UK but which have proved successful in the hands of development agencies in other parts of the world.

"The Board would be very glad to engage in constructive discussions with the aim of overcoming the real problems posed, for example by financial stringency, but unfortunately the only reaction is a series of alarmed objections on the lines of 'it's different, don't do it'.

"Again leaving aside the 'petro-chemical complex' the position is that you have been specifically asked whether any progress can be made on the major submissions from the Board and commercial companies on industrial developments or in the matter of natural resource exploration. The results have been so indecisive and such delay has been incurred as to produce a worse result than a straight 'no' would have done.

"Merely to indicate that this negative attitude is not confined to the Moray Firth, I would mention also a major land project in the Western Isles whose future is being prejudiced by a quite gratuitous difficulty introduced by the Scottish Office. Here again we have no signs of advance.

"I therefore tender my resignation from the Board forthwith in terms of schedule 1(4) of the Act. This is to protest at the attitude of the Scottish Office to Highland development. Furthermore I do not feel able to continue to take so substantial a salary from the public purse well knowing that the work done in return will merely be frustrated.

"May I say that I still hope that you will see your way to give real support to the Board which you have created but, if not, that you will take the appropriate steps on your part."

At his press conference at the end of the HIDB meeting Mr Ross, accompanied by Professor Grieve, said Mr Robertson's resignation was pretty well inevitable after the statements attributed to him, including the criticisms of the Scottish Office, civil servants and, by insinuation, the Secretary of State.

He criticised the rumours and speculation in which he said the Press had in the last week built stories about the Scottish Office rejection of the Invergordon project. It was nonsense to suggest there was opposition to the scheme in the Scottish Office; it had not been turned down for the simple reason no proposition had been made to them. He emphasised any proposition made had to be for consideration, examination and decision.

Professor Grieve stated the Board did not support Mr Robertson's views and did not associate themselves with them. However he bitterly regretted Mr Robertson's resignation. He was one of the most notable men with whom he had ever come in contact.

Remembering the 28th December, 1966 minute where he

insisted the Board must be 100% committed to support of Moray Firth Development and the petro-chemical complex project, that Board members must stand together and support each other and the Board's policy at all times, and that they were in fact committed to the hilt (see Appendix), his attitude seemed to offer further evidence of weakness, inadequacy and even disloyalty on the part of a Chairman faced with continued lack of political support and the active obstruction of Sir Douglas Haddow in Dover House.

At John Robertson's press conference he said the Board had pressed Mr Ross to declare in favour of Moray Firth Development in general and the Invergordon Chemical Complex in particular and, when they failed, he had resigned telling Mr Ross he should do the same. When he was told that the Occidental Petroleum Company had the previous day stated in a press conference that they were not prepared to make any proposition regarding Invergordon until they saw the Government attitude towards the scheme and was asked if he thought it was up to Government to take the first step, he replied "I do".

From the above it really did look like "after you Cecil; no, after you Claude". The Secretary of State now faced a most difficult situation. His brainchild was falling to bits and both he and Sir Matthew Campbell were perplexed and distressed by events. He had to face a debate in the House the following week and George Thomson was poised in the wings to replace him. I was phoned by Alasdair Mackenzie, unhappy that he was being criticised by the Liberal Party for having put up John Robertson for the board appointment.

I now drove down to London to await the Scottish Grand Committee debate. On Tuesday, 11th July Jane and I were in Westminster Hall before ten o'clock where we met Ian Grimble, and thence to the Committee Room where the Scottish Grand Committee were to meet. We all sat together, with Grieve and Fasken in the row behind and, while Ian was out, Hugh Fraser joined us.

During the first day of the debate Russell Johnson questioned land use techniques employed by the Board and how the Invergordon site had been selected by Frank Thomson, who was a friend of his; nevertheless he sought details of what he would gain should Occidental go ahead. Gordon Campbell, in a thoughtful speech on Highland development, emphasised his criticism was of Mr Ross and not of the Highland Board. Tony Stoddart laid emphasis on the importance of agriculture and, in particular, the rare resources of top quality land in the region.

When John Rankin, a Labour MP, rose to speak both Ian and Willie Ross left the chamber, as did Grieve who was present when Ross grabbed Grimble's tie to ask "Are you out to talk to the *Daily Express?*" Ian, ignoring Grieve, merely told him he welcomed the newly announced appointment of Sir James Mackay, a retired civil servant who had been responsible in the Home Office for prisons, and the Right Hon Tom Fraser, Chairman of the Hydro-Electric Board, to replace Robertson and Thomson.

The Secretary of State in answering matters raised in the first day claimed yet again that information had been passed to everyone but himself and criticised the disgraceful way the vendetta had been pursued. He flatly contradicted John Robertson's criticism of the Scottish Office in his resignation letter. He added that the Board and his department should not operate at arm's length, nor had they. While most Labour MPs did not acknowledge Ian, Tam Dalyell made a point of speaking to him, while I exchanged pleasantries with a rather embarrassed Robert Maclennan when we found ourselves alongside in the loo.

At the conclusion of the first day in the lobby outside I was questioned by a bevy of lobby correspondents, who ignored Grieve standing nearby – if looks could kill. Leaving the Palace of Westminster I needed a hand down the steps in my chair which was given by Willie Russell who represented the Scottish Office at Board meetings. Grieve and Fasken who were with him watched. Sitting beside Sybil Paterson on her flight north next day Jane saw

Grieve two seats behind and, when John Robertson joined the plane at Turnhouse, he sat with Grieve, exchanging notes and laughing during the brief flight to Dalcross.

In the second day of the debate Robert Maclennan spoke sensibly on land use; Malcolm Macmillan from the Western Isles supported the work of the Highland Transport Board now to be transferred to HIDB; Joe Grimond made the expected balanced and statesmanlike speech before Gordon Campbell summed up the case for the holding of a public inquiry into the Highland Board and the facts leading up to Thomson's resignation. On the defensive and answering hardly any of the questions raised in the two day debate the Secretary of State made a hectoring and lecturing speech, which Grimond later suggested to Ian added one more nail to his coffin, with Labour noticeably not even bothering to defend the Board's goings on. Apparently Dickson Mabon had told Maclennan to concentrate his speech on land use and not to bother to defend Ross. That afternoon I visited the *Sunday Times* office to discuss with James Evans, their legal advisor, the possible response to any libel claim from Thomson.

Unfortunately, because of a four-day press strike, no Scottish papers on the debate were printed till Friday when the *Glasgow Herald* published the article by Bill Williams headed 'Highland Board and Invergordon' which had been planned for the first day of the debate. In his article he criticised the Board's disregard of 'local conditions' and 'local needs' and the ineptitude of its public relations and reluctance to discuss openly its plans and projects, in particular the Invergordon petro-chemical scheme. Those questioning its wisdom had been accused of treachery, branded anti-Highland and assumed to be in the pocket of and in league with the 'wicked landlords'.

He suggested it was not unreasonable to doubt the scheme's profitability or the availability of a vast pool of skilled emigré labour south of Perth waiting for an opportunity to move north. He questioned the source of cheap power at far less cost per unit than the Central Electricity Generating Board or the Atomic Energy Authority could manage. He also questioned the claim made in the *Times* article of £10m of equity readily available from Scottish institutions. Further he thought that in the cold light of economic day the Invergordon scheme as we know it failed to convince.

Bill Williams continued by stating that any scheme could be made to pay – given sufficient Government backing. An ice cream factory on the summit of Ben Nevis could be made viable by a Government prepared to find free money to back it. There were competitive claims on Government finance; he instanced electrification of the main West Coast Glasgow to Crewe main line, or the building of a motorway between Glasgow and Edinburgh, or the improvement of Turnhouse airport. Should the Government really want to back the Highlands, how about a Highland research institute as a first step to a Highland university?

He ended his article to suggest no one in business could believe that an overnight transformation of a depressed area like the Highlands could be a remote possibility. HIDB would do well to prevent the area sinking into economic chaos. In its projected form each job created by the Invergordon development would cost over £6,000. By any reasonable standard this was too much to pay to give a man a job anywhere in Britain. The Highland developers must get back to their drawing board. This article articulated local concern about the petro-chemical scheme, no matter how unpopular locally such doubts might be.

We heard that, back in Inverness, Grieve had told his staff that, unpopular though he knew himself to be, he would be staying on as otherwise Ross, whom Scotland needed, would have to go. Soon after, Ross announced his refusal of Gordon Campbell's request to hold a public inquiry into the Board's recent activities. Then, early in August, we heard that a survey not authorised in HIDB minutes by Bechtel into electricity generation had not been accepted for payment and they were threatening to sue. Ian Grimble having travelled south with Joe Grimond wrote asking me to send him a brief history of the Board's involvement in the petro-chemical project and he later announced he was not interested in the HIDB chairmanship.

All Colin Campbell's friends were saddened to read advertisements for Forest Farm, Corriemuilzie and Drumvaith but relieved to hear Balblair was safe. Soon after Thomson's Rolls Royce, one of the assets of Ross-shire Engineering, had been transferred to the travel agents Duncan Duffy, owned by Thomson's family Trust, whose managing director Rene Duffy was later to resign. The proposal that creditors should accept shares in Ross-shire Engineering and continue trading despite losses of £37,000 in its last financial year was turned down. The company folded with a Board of Trade loan unredeemed. On 2nd October creditor's meetings were held for six of the Polyscot companies, including the controlling company, but excluding Polyscot Polycast which continued to trade for a time. So burst the Polyscot bubble.

Surprisingly, the *Glasgow Herald* invited me to write an article on how I believed it should act in the future. This appeared under their title "What needs done in Highlands". This is what I wrote:-

"When the Highlands and Islands Development Board was set up two years ago it began with the almost universal support and good will of the people of the seven crofter counties.

"The Board started with certain awkward disabilities. It was superimposed on an existing framework of numerous elected and appointed public bodies. For example, one of the principle disadvantages suffered by the region lay in high transport costs and the awkwardness of communications. Yet for the first 18 months the board was precluded from active consideration of transport problems.

"Again, the board needed to make its own plans but found itself subject to existing planning authority vested in the seven county councils.

"The Highland people have over the last six decades

developed an understandable suspicion of government. In the past timber had been cut for iron smelting, leaving the soil to erode. Sheep had been introduced to use the fertility built up by centuries of cattle and timber - they were more profitable than the natives, while barren hills a century later would be a problem for others.

"When the starving people became a nuisance a judge was sent and gave them security of tenure of their inadequate holdings. When this did not work a Crofters Commission was established under a man with a lifetime of colonial experience but little knowledge of the crofters and none of their language. After such experience it was natural that Highlanders were enthusiastic at being given their own development board.

"It was unfortunate there was no Gaelic speaker on the board. It was disappointing to find the top three staff to be civil servants of somewhat run of the mill experience and promotion. The finance available seemed inadequate, even before Selective Employment Tax hit the service industries of the region.

"The board began well with a couple of rapid rescue operations to aid a fish-processing firm in Shetland and a glassmaking business in Caithness. Its grants and loans scheme was well received, if ill publicised.

"A staff was engaged and soon the senior posts were advertised. Great numbers applied, the majority Highlanders. It became clear that Highlanders were not to be chosen: the necessary qualifications appeared to be experience in the colonies, in fact one of them had to ask which were the seven crofter counties. The advertisement for the tourist team originally appeared in the *New York Times*.

"More and more people seemed to be working at 6 Castle Wynd, Inverness and less and less information on their activities was made public. The island of Mull was disheartened by hearing a board member tell a farmer there at a public meeting that if he could not make a go of farming he had better get out and try something else. The whole island knew Forestry Commission men were active in their midst, but inquiries provoked the reply that no information could be given. Yet it was quite clear that a survey of plantable land was being made. The secrecy seemed pointless.

"Before the board was appointed the farming community had been heartened by the publication in 1964 of the Highland Panel's report *Land use in the Highlands and Islands*. Now there was a board able to encourage, aid and help finance more productive use of the lands.

"But it soon became clear that the board, under the wing of the Department of Agriculture for Scotland, believed existing agricultural subsidies took care of Highland agriculture and that its most useful activity lay in other fields, notably heavy industry and tourism. It did, however, aid one most necessary scheme to market calves reared in the Uists and Benbecula.

"Highlanders can produce saleable commodities in small and isolated communities but have little idea how to sell what is produced. The suggestion of a co-operative marketing organisation made in the report *Highland Opportunity* in 1964 does not seem to have found favour.

"Yet it seems possible that marketing help would expand many existing industries as well as encouraging others to start up. This would provide a far greater volume of employment for far less money than petro-chemical complexes. But really competent and experienced men would be needed to do the marketing if confidence is to be gained.

"The board made major industrial development its first priority and for over a year it has been concentrating on establishing an industrial complex in the Moray Firth area. Its plans have been made in secret, as far as is possible in a region where information flows freely.

"It now looks unlikely that Occidental Petroleum will build its petro-chemical complex at Invergordon and hope is transferred to obtaining the aluminium smelter that was to follow petro-chemicals. Indeed the board with this in view has committed more money to studies for heavy industrial development than it has paid out in grants to the whole of the rest of the Highlands.

"Before major developments on this scale take place investigations of geography, geology, transport, finance, amenity, and social effects of all alternative effects have to be made. Such surveys are impossible to carry out in secret. A site has now been chosen for the development on good arable land and an inquiry is to be held.

"Now seems the time for the board to publish the Moray Firth Industrial Credibility Study, the Bechtel Electricity Generating Study and the Jack Holmes Planning Group Infrastructure Study.

"The biggest failure at the board has been in its public relations. Members must become known to and confide in the Highland people. Letters must be acknowledged and answered promptly and proper reception facilities be provided for callers at the board's offices. Confidence must be regained so that planning for the future will be supported and helped.

"I believe the Highland Board should initiate land capability surveys so that land worth improving can be identified. It should examine the marketing of Highland products to try and improve its efficiency.

"It should look at transport facilities and discover where they are not being used. For example the MacBrayne car ferries to the islands are almost empty all winter. The service must be maintained. Very low rates for lorry loads would both increase the operator's income at no extra cost and benefit islanders: the present service appears designed to convenience mainlanders and tourists rather than islanders.

"A far closer link should be forged with councils of social service to discover the needs and problems of communities. The grants and loans available should be better publicised. The impression that the board prefers aid to go to those from outside must be contradicted. Only after people have been convinced that the first priority is to aid the indigenous population will the board be properly supported."

Chapter Ten
On to the Millennium

The first amendment to Ross & Cromarty County Council's Development Plan proposed to re-zone for industry only Inverbreakie Farm, Occidental and lCE's chosen site for its petro-chemical complex. This raised 23 objections, including one from Easter Ross Land Use Committee (ERLUC). They had already begun to consider how best to oppose development on top quality agricultural land before the planning consultant Alexander McIndoe had agreed to act for them. Somewhat ironically McIndoe had been replaced as Regional Planning Officer for the Highlands in St Andrew's House by Grieve. In case development on higher marginal land should prove uneconomic, he accepted it was worth investigating a possible alternative site beside deep water at the North Sutor entrance to the Cromarty Firth at Nigg, with some land reclamation from Nigg sands.

Confirming earlier rumours, Alcan (UK) stated their interest in building an aluminium smelter beside a coal-generated power station near Invergordon. Days later, British Aluminium announced they also were considering sites either in the north or south west of England or beside the Cromarty Firth. These announcements reinforced the need to find alternative sites off the best arable land

By early November, 1967 both aluminium companies had obtained options and applied for planning permission, BA at lnverbreakie, Occidental's chosen site, and Alcan at Ord which for 85 years had been the home farm of my in-laws. As a result of this change, Ord was added to the land to be re-zoned for industry.

At this time, at a meeting of the Scottish Peat and Land Development Association in Oban attended both by Prophet Smith of HIDB and Robert Maclennan MP, I questioned the MP as to whether it would be wrong to agree to put industry on top quality land before sites on poorer land had been investigated and eventually received the reply "Yes, it would be wrong", Smith adding that HIDB always examined alternatives but that developments of the Invergordon kind were primarily a matter for the industries concerned to choose.

My wife and brother-in-law, having jointly given an option on Ord, were advised it would be inappropriate for them to object to the Council's proposal to add Ord to industrially zoned land. Nothing more had been heard from Occidental. When the Chief Engineer of Alcan visited Ord he said, in answer to a question about John Robertson's position, that his company did not employ him though he was working closely with them. The farming community, after discovering the adverse effects of fluoride discharges from aluminium smelters causing bone defects and sometimes death in animals, investigated the compensation terms agreed at Fort William between British Aluminium and Mr Hobbs of the Great Glen Cattle Ranch.

Sandy McIndoe accepted my suggestion that I ask Tom Dowling, a talented artist who had served as navigator with me in **HMS/M Scorcher**, to draw a picture of a smelter and associated atomic power station built on land reclaimed from the sea at Nigg as an alternative industrial site. Contact was made with London consulting civil engineers experienced in suction-dredging land reclamation and, to represent ERLUC, an approach was made to Mr James Mackay, Q.C., with whom Jane and I had a discussion in a car on the banks of the Ness, before he found the timing of the public inquiry in February clashed with his other legal commitments withdrawing, later to rise to become Lord Chancellor. In his place Mr Archie Elliott Q.C. agreed to represent ERLUC. On Sandy's advice

Tom's aerial perspective and a press statement were issued ten days before the inquiry was due to start. This we later discovered had caused consternation to the amendment's promoters. By then B.A. had taken a further option on land to the north of Inverbreakie as a possible site for a bauxite plant, while Alcan took one on Kincraig House, now vacant after Polyscot's departure, as their headquarters.

Gathered in Ross & Cromarty's Dingwall council chamber, the Public Inquiry, chaired by Mr William Munro, Q.C., assisted by Mr McCamley from the Alkali Inspectorate and Mr Wallace from the Lands Department, got under way. The legal representatives present were to have distinguished careers: for the Council was Mr Johnson, later Lord Kincraig, assisted by Mr Edwards, later the British member of the European Court of Justice; for Alcan, Mr Jauncey, later to sit as a law lord in the House of Lords, assisted by Mr Cullen, later as Lord Cullen to hold Piper Alpha and Dunblane inquiries; while Mr Elliott, later Lord Elliott, for the objectors, was later to chair the Scottish Land Court.

Representing myself, working among them, I discovered how enjoyable I found the cut and thrust of examination and cross examination, which fifteen years later I would exercise in Citizens Advice Bureau representation of clients in Employment and Social Security Tribunals. I learned about leading questions, how to avoid them and how, on occasion, an amateur might, before being stopped, help a witness not performing as hoped.

I felt it politic not to cross-examine the first witness, Professor Grieve, giving evidence for the Highland Board who had so publicly sacked me a year earlier, enjoyable though it might have been. His evidence was followed by that of the council, marine experts, and representatives of both aluminium companies. Then it was the objectors' turn and Elliott questioned McIndoe, two consulting engineers, a Dutchman from Bos & Kalis, reclamation experts, who offered a trip to Holland sponsored by their associates, the Westininster Dredging Company, to see suction dredging in progress, followed by farming experts.

Only then did individual objectors get their turn. After I had concluded my evidence the Reporter was kind enough to say. "Thank you very much Mr Durham, that is a most eloquent speech you have made, and I think even Counsel could hardly have bettered that."

On the last day the inquiry was interrupted by bagpipes and loud hailers from a large procession of protesting local unemployed workers and their families, transported to Dingwall in buses, which it was rumoured were paid for by Alcan. Only when, after some delay, they agreed to accept the Reporter's invitation to allow a representative to give evidence on their behalf was the inquiry able to proceed. When participants summed up it became clear that the evidence given by ERLUC's witnesses upset planners and aluminium producers alike. They argued that using a level site provided by reclamation at Nigg would be cheaper than those chosen. Though their site required large scale levelling they argued that there was no time to allow a survey of the suitability of Nigg Bay for reclamation.

Soon a company, Grampian Chemicals, announced they planned petro-chemical development in the area. This would later lead to even more extensive proposed zoning of agricultural land for industry. However, this account first summarises the birth and death of the British Aluminium smelter on Inverbreakie.

The proposed establishment of two, later to become three, aluminium smelters in Britain involved some form of subsidy of electricity cost, contrary to an EFTA agreement not to give such subsidies, smelting being one of the most power intensive industries. Protest by Norway, with its large aluminium industry powered by cheap hydro-electric power, was disregarded but did delay the fmal decision till the end of July, by which time the rezoning had been approved, but not before my father-in-law, still unwilling to accept the destruction of his farm, had died.

Alcan having been persuaded to build their smelter and coal burning power station over a coal mine at Blyth in Northumberland, the successful company British Aluminium required to use a strip of Ord marching with Inverbreakie to build its smelter. This led to negotiations with both companies on the relinquishing of Alcan's option and allowing BA to replace them. This gave Jane with her brother a chance to delay agreement until the company accepted the establishment of an NFU/BA liaison committee to agree compensation for any loss suffered by farmers from the effects of fluorosis caused by discharges from the plant.

Later, two farmers were forced to change their farming methods, one to abandon a dairy and the other a single-suckling beef herd. Armed with the results of weekly herbage sampling at 31 sites, the compensation agreement worked well, with goodwill on both sides. While taking our eldest son out for his Charterhouse midsummer break, I had managed to visit the Central Veterinary Laboratory in Woking to spend half an hour with antipodean Mrs Allcroft, a world expert who had co-authored the two volume treatise *Fluorosis in Cattle* and this had greatly helped the drafting of the agreement.

BA's Invergordon smelter power contract was based on an estimated, but never achieved, electricity cost from partly built Hunterston B advanced gas-cooled atomic reactor and BA was voted a £30m. Board of Trade loan at a fixed interest rate of 7% repayable in 28 years. From May, 1971 when the first potline opened during a world slump in aluminium prices, there followed over the next ten years a rectiformer fire, a strike, then a severe snowstorm causing three of the four power supply lines to fail. Eventually through a Hunterston worker opening a wrong valve to allow sea water to enter Hunterston B's cooling system, by then part of BA's property, the smelter was forced to shut down after just ten years' production. Built partly piled and partly rafted, the pot rooms' instability caused such vibration that the large fans beneath each of the six chimneys required several replacements, such fans lasting for decades elsewhere.

The rise and fall of the British Aluminium Invergordon smelter proved a classic example of the folly of Government promotion and indirect subsidy of an economically unsound industry for political reasons. Most countries blessed with large bauxite deposits wisely add value to their resource by themselves processing it into aluminium for export. The failure added 700 unemployed workers to a predominantly rural area, while food production from the farmland on which it had been built was destroyed for ever.

Next in the queue to build heavy industry on good arable farmland was the newly established Grampian Chemicals, largely financed by an American oil prospecting company, Planet Oil. Its chairman, Eoin Mekie, having failed to set up a vast development at Milford Haven which had gone bust owing around £1m, had transferred his interest to the Cromarty Firth, joined by Angus Morrison with oil and chemical industry experience and, popping up once again, Dr Jonathan Jenkins, still working for HIDB but now only outside the Moray Firth. There were no other employees and the business was conducted from a residential flat in London. They proposed to build a chemical complex on Delny Farm, bought from the chairman of the Ross & Cromarty Planning Committee, with a pipe line across an adjoining farm and Nigg Bay sands to Nigg, where a deep-water terminal would load its products, mainly coke, of which they claimed a world shortage.

As a result of their application, the local authority planned to add a further 1025 acres to the industrially zoned land. Following a further 18-day public inquiry in March 1969, Mr O'Brien, QC, recommended the Secretary of State to refuse the proposal. In his report the Reporter doubted if, in accordance with Regulation 5 of the Town and Country Planning Regulations, the County Council had properly consulted the Agricultural Executive Committee before preparing their amendment to the County development plan. Despite Mr O'Brien's advice, Willie Ross approved the amendment, in effect saying "Don't muddle me with the facts; my mind is made up". However the objectors appealed the legality of the failure to consult the AEC so that in March 1970 the First Division of the Inner House of the Court of Session held a hearing in Edinburgh's Parliament House. Lords Clyde, Migdale and Milligan mounted their throne above assembled clerks, advocates and solicitors with, behind, members of public and press, to consider for three days the meaning of three words: *consult, before* and *planning*.

Much argument focused about when a plan was prepared and on the difference between consulting and telling. The dozen of us down from the North, with Sandy McIndoe in attendance, formed the opinion after the second day that their lordships leant towards Archie Elliott's claim that Mr O'Brien had been correct in suggesting that the Agricultural Executive were not consulted, merely told, about the proposed amendment. However, their attitudes appeared to change overnight so that on the third day they found that the County Council had not broken the law. Fatefully that very day Grampian Chemicals went into liquidation. Once more Robertson and Jenkins appeared thwarted, though they did set up in partnership a chemical company, J & R Hykem, of their own. Now a County Councillor, John Robertson's proposal to establish a quarry on his ground did, however, meet considerable environmental opposition. One objector was obliged to resign from her County Council employment because she wrote to the press. To house incoming workers, sixty acres of land at Alness was approved for new housing, part of the good farm of Culcraggie being rejected for this purpose.

The 1971 discovery of North Sea oil at last provided for Easter Ross a solid large scale industry using indigenous resources. Highlands Fabricators were given virtually unopposed permission to dig their big hole at Nigg, on the very site the farmers had suggested for a smelter at the first public inquiry; while, on the other side of the Moray Firth, Macdermotts started to build a competing dry-land rig construction yard at Ardesier, the two yards later to combine. To bring the oil ashore pipes were needed, so pipe coating and manufacturing yards developed on the unused Ord land, at Evanton and the Morrich Moor disused aerodrome. Once more the planners, encouraged by HIDB, became over excited, drawing up plans, later withdrawn, to provide a settlement in the countryside housing 60,000 new inhabitants at Lamington, as well as expansion of housing in the three towns of Tain, Invergordon and Alness and beside the rural villages of Milton and Seaboard.

Because all this development involved greater shipping use of the firth, a Port Authority was set up, replacing the Admiralty as harbour authority, but its ambition to achieve compulsory purchase rights was thwarted by Parliamentary Commissioners, after a hearing chaired by Lord Selkirk. At last, following no fewer than four public inquiries, the planners seemed content, with spare land for housing, three good arable farms zoned for industrial use but still farmed and the poor land at Nigg also available. The land use committee could relax. Peace was not to be enjoyed for long.

In 1973 a new firm, Cromarty Petroleum, owned by reputedly the world's richest man, following the deaths of Howard Hughes and Paul Getty, bought the Grampian land on which to build a refinery and chemical complex. Daniel K. Ludwig with his Universe Tankships and National Bulk Carriers, was an even larger owner of Liberian-registered bulk ore carriers and super-tankers than the Greeks Onassis and Niarchos. This time it was the likely environmental effects not land use that were to split the local community. No one was surprised to find Dr Jonathan Jenkins based in Cromarty Petroleum's London office as their European agent, or that John Robertson, Jenkins's partner in J & R Hykem, and owning land at Nigg would prove the company's strongest spokesman for Support Cromarty Oil Terminal (SCOT) battling for public support against Cromarty Refinery Opposition Workers (CROW). Once more the community was deeply divided.

The decision of the Planning Committee not to grant planning permission was reversed at a later meeting but, after they sought a direction by the Secretary of State under Article 8 of Planning Law, Willie Ross decided to hold what proved the longest running Public Inquiry ever to be held in Scotland. Over eight weeks in the spring of 1975 the future Lord Chancellor James McKay, Q.C., led no fewer than 30 expert witnesses for the granting of planning permission before a further 30 gave evidence against. As the then President of the local NFU, I found myself wearing two different hats, able to cross-examine each witness twice. Jane, who had done considerable research into Ludwig and his past activities and into American experience of and research into the effects of oil spills, concluded her evidence in her brief summing up statement: "The character of Mr Ludwig is still shrouded in mystery, which does not inspire sufficient confidence to justify leaving the future of our environment in his hands. I do not consider our democratic defences are strong enough to afford protection against the risk of future exploitation at the whim of one elderly American gentleman."

It took Mr Maycock the Reporter seven months to consider the 6,500 foolscap pages of evidence and produce his report, which recommended that the Secretary of State refuse planning permission. In March 1976 Willie Ross yet again failed to accept his Reporter's recommendation and authorised the Council to give the go ahead, subject to stringent planning conditions. Unfortunately for Ludwig he was unable to purchase the strip of land essential to building his deep water berths, the owners being willing only to offer a lease. After that, refused a compulsory purchase order by the local authority, the company was forced to promote its own parliamentary order to try to acquire its vital access.

In Edinburgh, Parliamentary Commissioners passed on the Cromarty Petroleum Order for consideration by the House of Commons. Such an order under rarely used private legislation procedures would often be passed 'on the nod' without debate but not this time; it was blocked by Jeff Rooker, a Labour M.P. and, after a three hour debate in October, the Bill was talked out. Only late in 1976, did Highland Regional Council, by this time the responsible planning authority, authorise a Compulsory Purchase Order. By then Beatrice Field, a deposit of thick waxy oil, had been discovered off Helmsdale in the Moray Firth. It was eventually to be piped to a tank farm to the north of Highlands Fabricators yard and then loaded by a pier out on the deep channel. Speculation was rife and local inhabitants watched the price of a 500 acre sandbank on Nigg Sands rise from fifty thousand pounds to £1.3 million in a few months. Dow Chemicals, the eventual owner, had beaten off two other potential refinery developers, Highland Hydrocarbons and British Gas Corporation.

The tide still floods the sandbank twice a day, while Ludwig's complex was never built.

Indeed, when Highland Regional Council proposed a new structure plan in 1980, Mr Maycock was back to hold an Examination in Public of its proposals, at which I was invited to attend by the Secretary of State, and where was revealed the two-year suppression of a report by Cremer & Warner on pollution dangers of petro-chemical development at Nigg where three settlements at Cromarty. Milton and Barbaraville fell within the US danger fall-out zone.

Various Dutchmen bought property in Easter Ross before, most of them, departing whence they came, one of them via Perth Prison. The harbour at Invergordon has expanded to offer three simultaneous berths for oil rigs under repair, while still able to handle over thirty visits a year from even the largest cruise liners. Since the closure of the British Aluminium smelter in 1981 inhabitants have been able to enjoy our remarkable clarity of clean, unpolluted air. Within seven miles of my home, Scotsburn, lie four malt distilleries, Balblair, Glenmorangie, Dalmore and Teaninich, as well as the enormous Invergordon Grain distillery.

While local prosperity has depended heavily on the success of its largest local employer, Highlands Fabricators, to win orders, many smaller local companies producing anything from nail varnish to smoked fish have developed, quite apart from two call centres employing over 500 mainly female workers each. Daniel Defoe's 'noble harbour' has replaced its grey lines of moored warships by cumbersome oil drilling rigs resting or under repair, lit after dark like gigantic Christmas trees.

Appendix

AN EXAMINATION OF THE ACTIVITIES OF THE
HIGHLANDS AND ISLANDS DEVELOPMENT BOARD, OF
ITS PART-TIME MEMBER, FRANK G. THOMSON, AND OF
THE BUSINESSES IN WHICH HE TAKES AN ACTIVE PART.

Some of Mr Thompson's business interests.

"In August, 1965, partly as a result of the unpublished Part II
of a report by Martech Consultants carried out for the Scottish
Vigilantes Association, Part I of which was published in October,
1965 as 'Highland Opportunity', Mr Frank G Thomson and Mr
Colin J Campbell formed a series of companies of the Polyscot
Group namely: Polyscot Ltd; Polyscot Agencies Ltd; Polyscot
Farm Supplies Ltd; Polyscot Finance Ltd; Polyscot Polycast Ltd;
Polyscot Properties Ltd; Timber Systems Ltd; and two associated
companies: Ross-shire Engineering Ltd and, later, Uniscot (C.N.)
Ltd.

"A further company, Invergordon Chemical Enterprises, Ltd
was set up as a shell company later and its name-plate appeared on
the outside of Kincraig House beside the name-plates of the other
Polyscot Group Companies.

"Mr Thomson and his wife have, in addition, a venture in
station refreshment rooms at Braemar and Dingwall, and he and his

125

brother have a property development company to develop a site in the middle of Aberdeen.

"Recently, Mr and Mrs Thomson bought a controlling interest in Duncan Duffy, the long established travel agents in Inverness.

"When the Polyscot Group Companies were established, the County Development Officer of Sutherland, Mr Douglas Fasham, resigned and joined Messrs Thomson and Campbell.

Grants and Loans made and pending from the Highlands and Islands Development Board to Mr Thomson's companies.

"In March, 1966, the month Mr Thomson joined the Board as a part time Member, the Board made a grant to Polyscot of £1,500. for a building at Mr Campbell's farm, Balblair, Bonar Bridge, Sutherland, which was already erected, and a loan of £23,500. at 5.5%. The Board insisted on the two directors making joint and several guarantees for the loan as the bank references, which were sealed by the secretary of the Board from further scrutiny.

The statement submitted with the application was as follows:-

ASSETS		LIABILITIES	
Issued Capital	40,000	Fixed Assets	17,337
Revenue deficit	54,478 15 10		
Deficiency of assets	14,478 15 10	Associated companies	16,355
		Debtors	7,149
Owing Creditors	12,355		
Bank	38,822		
Directors	4,142		
	55,319		
	£40,841		£40,841

This grant had been paid by the 12th May, 1966.

"A further application for financial assistance, this time for Ross-Shire Engineering (Dingwall) Ltd was submitted in August. This company, in which the Polyscot Group has the major voting power, has a loan of £20,000 from the Board of Trade and overdraft facilities from the Bank of £10,000.

"Security for these advances was by floating charge on the assets of the company, the total value of whose assets was £34,000. This left practically no security available for any loan which might be available from the Board. The company required between £15,000 and £25,000 to buy new plant and machinery and for working capital.

"The issued capital of the company was £75,000 of which 30% is held by Polyscot Ltd. The directors were Mr Frank Thomson (Chairman), Mr C. Campbell, Mr A. Morrison, Building Contractor, Tain, Ex-Provost Macrae, Dingwall, and Mr W. Duncan, Solicitor, Inverness.

"The Ross-shire Engineering Company (Dingwall) Ltd, has been having trading losses since its inception and in the first six months of 1966 the trading loss was £6,000 with a predicted loss for the whole year of £12,000.

"After the Secretariat recommended rejection of this application, it was dropped temporarily.

"On 10th November, 1966 a tendering fee of £300 was paid to Polyscot to offer draft plans and sketch elevations on which a realistic approximate quotation for building 5 motel/hotels @ £200,000 each could be based. It was suggested that it would be only right that the Board should explore the possibilities of one or more of these hotels being constructed in the Highlands by a Highland firm. No similar tendering fee was offered to British Aluminium who are also based in the Highlands.

"The application for assistance to Ross-Shire Engineering (Dingwall) Ltd has not been dropped and an attempt is being made to have £23,800 voted to them, despite a recommendation by the Secretariat that this application be rejected.

Invergordon Chemical Enterprises Ltd.

"The first public reference to this company was made by the Member of the Board responsible for Moray Firth Development, Mr John Robertson, in a speech to the Ross & Cromarty County Council in Dingwall on Wednesday, 18th January, 1967. It is interesting that this speech varied from the approved text handed out to the Press who complained about this at the press conference afterwards.

"All that is known about Invergordon Chemical Enterprises Ltd is that it was registered with two one-pound shares by two subscribers. It is known that its name plate is on the door of Kincraig House, the headquarters of the Polyscot Group, that at the Board Meeting which appointed Mr John Robertson in charge of the Moray Firth Project Mr Frank Thomson was appointed to assist on Moray Firth Project including liaison with ICE. Recent meetings of the Moray Firth Progress Group have been attended by Mr Douglas Fasham on behalf of ICE.

Martech consultants, Product Planning, ICE and the Board.

"Martech Consultants and Product Planning Ltd (Proplan) are two companies in the Sigma Group of International Consultants. Amongst the employees of Proplan up to the end of January 1967 was Dr Jonathan Jenkins, D.Sc.

"While Mr Thomson was still Managing Director of Invergordon Distillers Ltd, a company controlled by Mr Max Rayne's London Merchant Securities, and as a follow-on of an examination of possible uses of surplus carbon dioxide from Invergordon Distillery in Part II of a report made for the Scottish Vigilantes, Chairman Frank Thomson, a feasibility study for the establishment of a petro-chemical complex was commissioned from Proplan. The instructions to make this study were on Invergordon Distillers paper, signed by the managing director, Mr Thomson. Some of the subsequent correspondence was on Polyscot paper, but it would appear that the responsibility for payment for this study, which cost £55,000, is Invergordon Distillers'.

"In April, 1966, just subsequent to Mr Thomson's appointment to the Board, there was a row with Mr Rayne and Mr Thomson was sacked and Mr Boyd was appointed in his place. Initially Mr Rayne announced that Mr Thomson would remain in an advisory capacity, but by the end of June Mr Thomson's association with Invergordon Distillers Ltd terminated and, a week later, he left for eight weeks in the US.

"When, in March, Mr Frank Thomson joined the Board, he brought with him the three-volume report by Proplan 'Chemical Complex at Invergordon, Feasibility Study' dated October,1965. At the first meeting he attended on 18th March, 'Mr Thomson described to the Board the course of the most recent developments towards the development of a petro-chemical complex. It was agreed after discussion that it was essential that, in the timing of operations, action by the commercial interests should be matched by action by the Board in the area in which they could help.' At the next meeting a fortnight later 'The Board agreed to the action proposed by the Chairman and also to the suggestion that in carrying out this assignment Proplan should work from the Board office.' Already the consultants working for 'commercial interests' had been engaged to work for the Board. As will be seen later, the dividing line between work for 'commercial interests' and work for the Board was soon to become elastic except that the Board did all the paying. On 6th April, it was announced at a Board meeting that Proplan had agreed to undertake preliminary general survey work at a fee of £4,000 and that work on the survey, which it was hoped to complete in six weeks, had already commenced. There was only one snag: Proplan had not been paid for the original survey. After failing to obtain any money, two directors of the firm came to Invergordon in March to demand payment of the £55,000 and they left with a cheque for £17,500 signed by Mr Thomson on an Invergordon Distillers' cheque book. By November 1966, only

£24,000 remained outstanding, but it is not clear who paid the £13,500. However, what is known is that Mr Boyd, who took over the Managing Director's job at Invergordon Distillers on July 1st, approached the Board a fortnight later, just subsequent to Mr Thomson's departure for the States, and stated that he assumed the Board had accepted full responsibility for the feasibility study commissioned by Invergordon Distillers as he had been told they were in possession of it and were, indeed, doing more work on it. As a result of this, the study was posted off that night back to Invergordon Distillers in a registered envelope. The actual copy was of no importance for was not Mr Jenkins who wrote much of it working for the Board on other work at that very moment as the scientist on the Proplan team? Further, did not Mr Thomson have several other copies in Kincraig House, the headquarters of all his companies?

"The Proplan 'Credibility Study' entitled 'Development of the Moray Firth Area' was presented to the Board at a meeting on 18th August attended by Mr Willis, Minister of State for Scotland. Dr Jenkins addressed this meeting and explained how essential it was to have great quantities of electricity available at less than a halfpenny per unit.

"On 10th, 12th and 13th September a series of meetings were held with three representatives of the Rexall/Occidental Consortium. Dr Jenkins was present throughout. One meeting was held in Kincraig House and representatives of Ross & Cromarty County Council were met on the afternoon of 12th September. It was decided that the Chairman of the Development Board and Mr Thomson should visit America and that Dr Jenkins would be sent before and remain after them. In a record of this series of meetings 'Mr Robertson suggested that action be taken along the following lines:- first of all the Board had already received a letter of intent from Dr Hammer of Occidental. Going on from this the Board should receive an assurance from Rexall and Occidental that they were undertaking a site feasibility study followed by a financial feasibility study. For their part the Board would study the matter of freight rates, port development, etc; in this connection it was possible for the Board to acquire land at a figure of £200 to £300 an acre.' Thus some of the finest arable land in Scotland, never mind the Highlands, can be made available to American business men.

"On 17th September the Board re-organised their duties and Mr Robertson was appointed in charge of Moray Firth Project and Mr Thomson to assist on Moray Firth Project, including liaison with ICE.

"On 22nd September ' The Secretary reported that in addition to amounts already approved by the Board, Messrs Proplan were due fees amounting to £1,872:10:- for attendance at various meetings between the Board and industrialists. The Board authorised payment of this sum.' The interesting thing about this item is that Dr Jenkins's time was charged at £70 per day plus full expenses.

"On 29th September ' Mr J.C. Robertson asked Secretariat to make a provision, such that all monies expended in the development of the petro-chemical complex could be maintained, in order that Company formation expenses could be allocated at a later date. The Board agreed to a fee of up to £2,600 for Proplan Ltd, as outlined in Secretariat Paper No 150. The Deputy Chairman remarked that no details of the survey specification had been made available.' S.P. 150 states that, in preparation for a visit of the Chairman and Mr Thomson to Los Angeles, a comprehensive fund of information would require to be built up. Proplan were to study the Invergordon site and work out the possible output of the complex, distribution of the products, transport needs and the stages of development of the harbour, etc. It was expected that the Proplan team would consist of Dr Jenkins and one other consultant. Fees for the exercise would be £50 per day for Dr Jenkins working four days per week for the three weeks to 21st October, plus his expenses for the visit to America - say £2,000 in total. The fee for the other consultant would be £40 per day for pay, 15 consultant days up to a guaranteed maximum of £600.

"It is interesting to see that Dr Jenkins's fees have fallen £20 per day. However even £50 per day is quite useful. In October, 1966 the first Proplan survey was ready. It was entitled 'Survey of Fertiliser Distribution' and contains maps and details of how the future competitors of the Americans went about distributing their fertilisers and then continued with suggestions how the future complex should distribute its products to compete with ICI, Fisons and Shell. Thus a British Government is paying for a study how a foreign firm is to compete with British firms in their own market. The second study followed in November 1966 headed 'Mix Survey'. This was to a large extent technical but does state that the firm of Adam Lithgoe are to sell the fertilisers made by the complex. A study of Lithgoe's methods could be revealing. The firm who hope to distribute and sell at least 400,000 tons of fertiliser annually advertised for agents in Scotland, received over a score of replies, told the applicants that the job would go, as their sales representative, to the man who, unpaid, brought in most business by the end of the month and then, after receiving the orders of all the applicants, engaged none of them but merely fulfilled the orders. This is the chosen firm to sell American fertilisers in competition with British firms.

"In October 1966, Rexalls withdrew from the consortium and, at a meeting held in Claridges Hotel with five directors of Occidental Petroleum Corp. and a director of International Ore and Fertilisers (U.K.) Ltd, Professor Grieve, J.C. Robertson, F.G. Thomson, Dr Jenkins (Proplan on behalf of the Board) and the Secretary gave the following assurances:-

(1) The Government would give a 40% investment grant on plant and machinery;

(2) The Government would give a 35% building grant;

(3) The proposal for a Government loan of half the balance of cost after payment of the above-mentioned grants was a reasonable one and would be supported by the Board to the Government as

soon as the financial feasibility study was ready;

(4) The question of a moratorium on interest payments and capital requirements would form part of the discussion of the Government loan;

(5) Civil and Industrial infrastructure including housing, water supply, sewage, schools, hospitals, roads would be provided by the Government;

(6) The provision of adequate port facilities at Invergordon (the cost of which would be met from the public sector) would be pursued by the Board immediately;

(7) The Board are already involved in a comprehensive investigation to determine which of several technical methods of generating cheap electricity was the best for Invergordon;

(8) The Board were making detailed enquiries on the whole question of freight including charges. Their information to date already made it clear that freight would present no problem;

(9) The Board would ensure that ample labour of the right quality was available.

"Thus at Claridge's Hotel on 11th October the Board had committed the Government, with or without their approval, to finance the 'Civil and Industrial infrastructure' if the Americans decide to come.

"Before examining the Board's later decisions, it might be as well to complete the story of Dr Jenkins and Proplan. Dr Jenkins is leaving Proplan and has been given a one-year contract by the Board to start February 12th. His contract is for twelve days work per month and he is to be paid £40 per day plus all expenses. This is the highest salary of any member or employee of the Board except the Chairman. Presumably Dr Jenkins has decided that the complex will come off and that he has had all the good he can get out of Proplan. No one can blame him in view of the way all the costs of establishing Invergordon Chemical Enterprises are being paid by the Board. For all we know he may even be a future director of Invergordon Chemical Enterprises. Besides, £40 per day that he keeps himself is almost certainly better value to him than his employers getting £70 or £50 but only passing him his salary.

Kincraig House, the headquarters of the Polyscot Group and Invergordon Chemical Enterprises.

"Nine partners, one of them Frank Thomson, bought Kincraig Farm in 1964. Mr Thomson promised the others that the firm of Polyscot would rent the large mansion house as its headquarters. After Polyscot had rented Kincraig House for just over a year, Mr Thomson agreed to purchase it, the stables, a cottage occupied by Mr Douglas Fasham and ten acres of land for £15,000 to be paid on 29th November, 1966. On this understanding the National Commercial Bank of Scotland made a short-term loan to the partnership to be repaid at the end of November, 1966.

As Mr Thomson was in America at the Board's expense, his partner Mr Campbell was supposed to hand over the cheque. The cheque was not delivered, Mr Thomson failed to attend a meeting held to find out why he had not paid or even to send apologies and he finally wrote to the Chairman of the partnership, Mr Douglas Budge, as follows:-

'It has become more and more obvious to me that there will be increasing difficulties in my playing an objective and public-spirited role in my activities as a Member of the Highland Development Board, and at the same time retaining a partner's interest in Kincraig, which is situated generally in the area of potential development in the Cromarty Firth. I may say also at this time, in view of my Highland Development activities, that I have deemed it appropriate in the public interest not to proceed as an investor for private gain in the proposed Chemical Complex. You, and the rest of my partners in the land consortium, will, I am sure, appreciate that I will be placing myself in a most invidious position should I be directly associated with profit-making in either land or any other investment directly associated with the Moray Firth

industrialisation.

In view of these changed circumstances, and also my increasing awareness of the feelings regarding land in the Invergordon area, it will be necessary to have an early meeting to restate my whole position regarding Kincraig, and all other matters relevant to our business hitherto.'

"At a meeting held in Lower Kincraig, Mr Thomson said that the strong feelings about land had been made clear from letters to *The Scotsman* and Government authority. There had been criticism of his position by persons in authority. As a result he had given an undertaking to the Minister and the Board that he would not be concerned with land in the area. Partners would realise that Kincraig had been tied in with the long term liquidity of his operations. He had wished for the immediate sale of the house and the surrounding land to go through and he did not wish in any way to manoeuvre or manipulate. He had not left Britain with the intention of not paying the money over. He would hate partners to think that. But he found himself in an embarrassing situation. Kincraig House was now not only a liability but a public embarrassment too. If he moved out it would be at considerable loss as the house was intended to be the headquarters of the whole industrial development. It was quite unsuitable for Polyscot's operations and indeed Polyscot was going to move to Ross-Shire Engineering's works. The Chairman pointed out to Mr Thomson that they were committed to pay back the Bank. Mr Thomson said he was in a most dangerous position. He could, of course, step out of the Highland Development Board and take fat gains, but he was not interested in this. In any case, he believed that even if he were to pay the £15,000 Kincraig would lack liquidity. His lacking cheque was only part of the problem. The Chairman denied this and said that, although the overdraft was £46,000, the realisation of £22,000 from various sales would put the whole situation right from the farming point of view.

Mr Thomson said that if they insisted on his paying he would sell right away. In any case he must withdraw from the consortium. They really must realise the seriousness of his position. Mr Mann, Inverbreakie had written an open letter accusing him of being a party to land speculation. Other letters had been sent to the Minister of State and 10 Downing Street. He could not put the Board under pressure. One thing that had already been pointed out to him was that he could not be involved in gain due to the complex.

"Mr Thomson suggested that the Kincraig partners should try and get their money out of the Highland Development Board. They should approach Mr John Robertson and ask for a meeting with him and the Secretary, Mr Fasken. Mr Thomson said that whatever they did he must be clear by the evening of Monday, 9th January (two days later) and must have written confirmation to this effect.

"The partners told Mr Thomson they would not give him his certificate and they would take legal advice and the meeting then broke up. It is interesting to note that at a special Board meeting on 19th December, 1966, the following had already been proposed: 'The question of land for industrial sites at Invergordon to be considered urgently. Suggestions were that Mr Thomson might sell his existing land to Board at original purchase price; Board might take options on land for industrial use.' It would indeed be most interesting to know how and by whom these suggestions were made at this Board meeting. (See below).

Attempts at appointment of Polyscot partners to various boards.

"During the early summer of 1966 an unsuccessful attempt was made by Mr Thomson to get his co-director Mr Colin Campbell appointed to the Highland Development Board. Mr Campbell was so sure of success that he gave this further possible appointment as his reason for resigning from the Moray Firth Association, a land use group of which he was Chairman. He stated that he would be of more benefit to the Association from within the Board.

"In January 1967, an attempt was made to get Mr Thomson appointed to the North of Scotland Hydro-Electric Board. Mr Thomson's partner in Ross-Shire Engineering, ex-Provost Macrae is on this Board and hopes to join the Highland Development Board. Both attempts have failed so far.

The position of the Highlands and Islands Development Board and the Government

"It has been pointed out (at Claridges Hotel) that the Board had committed the Government to giving very substantial support if Occidental Petroleum Co. decide to come to Invergordon. The special meeting of the Board, subsequent to their member's trip to America, at which they decided to make a formal submission to the Secretary of State, makes the Board's total commitment to Mr Frank Thomson and to Invergordon Chemical Enterprises clear. All the Board members except Mr Scholes were present, as were Fasken, Spaven and Skewis of the Staff.

"At this meeting Members were told, as the Secretary of State was to be at the end of December, of the written agreement with Dr Hammer, President of the Occidental Petroleum Corporation, which Mr Thomson had brought back with him. Briefly this provided that :-

(1) Occidental would commission a preliminary feasibility study by H.W Kellogg Company of the petro chemical project to be completed by 31st March, 1967. This study, which has already been commissioned from H.W.Kellogg, together with marketing studies which Occidental propose to undertake, could cost up to $300,000 and would be paid by Occidental to match the expenditure on the project to date by Mr Thomson and the Board.

(2) Occidental would advise Mr Thomson by 1st June, 1967 whether it had decided to proceed with the project in whole or part.

(3) The Board would "use their best efforts to procure all

governmental approvals .... including the acts to be performed by the United Kingdom ...." <u>If such approvals were not obtained by 31st December, 1967,</u> there would be no obligation on Occidental to contribute any capital or participate in the project.'

'Mr Robertson said that given this timetable (and Kellogg's feasibility study team will be arriving at Invergordon on 16th January, 1967) the Board must be absolutely clear that they were 100% in support of Moray Firth Development and the Petro-Chemical Complex project. Given this extent of commitment on both sides of the Atlantic, now was the very last opportunity for the Board to withdraw without serious loss of face and without causing grievous embarrassment and damage to the Highland and National interest. In their consideration, members should bear in mind that M.F.D. meant a great change in their own parish and raised two big issues - <u>industry on good agricultural land</u> and <u>competition with other British industries.</u>'

'The Chairman then explained at length and in detail to the meeting what this would and could involve for the Board and individual Board members. He stressed that if any member had doubts or reservations about the Moray Firth concept they must be expressed now; the same went for the petro-chemical project; if the Board decided to go ahead, Members must stand together and support each other and the Board's policy at all times.'

'The ensuing discussion revealed that there was complete agreement among Members that the Moray Firth Development was an essential key in the Board's development strategy and that this concept should be pursued by the Board to the limit of their strength and powers.

'This was best summed up by Mr Smith who pointed out that at a special meeting on 17th September, 1966 the Board had already expressed fundamental agreement with the Moray Firth Development, that they were in fact committed to the hilt. It would be daft for the Board to limit themselves to catching the odd sprat if they could catch a whale. The whale would be bound to thresh about a bit but if it could be landed everything else the Board were doing or attempting to do would fade into insignificance.'

'The meeting next agreed the following action and detailed who was to be responsible in each section. The details have only been given here in Land, Power and Finance.

1. Alerting Government
2. Infrastructure planning
3. Water and Sewerage
4. Land   Action
   (a) Mr Spaven's responsibility
   (b) The question of land for industrial sites at
   Invergordon to be considered urgently. Suggestions were that
   Mr Thomson might sell his existing land to Board at original
   purchase price; Board might take options on land for
   industrial use.
5. Railways
6. Docks
7. Power   Board must have expert advice on questions of
   cheap power. There were two possibilities - a firm such as
   Bechtel which might eventually construct (and possibly
   finance) the power station and a firm of consultant engineers.
       Action A firm of consultants would be engaged.
8. Finance As regards the need for cheap power, Mr Robertson
explained that the initial case of ICE did not appear to be a
major consumer of electricity, most of the plant being operated
by steam raised by its own processes However further
development of the Complex would involve major arc furnaces
installation which might amount to 250mw for which cheap
power would be of the essence. An immediate major need for
power could, however, arise if the arc furnace method of
producing phosphoric acid were chosen in preference to the old
established but lower quality wet acid process. Immediately
cheap power would attract other industries, particularly

aluminium processors. They would have the great advantage of assuring ICE they would not be alone in their enterprise at Invergordon. However there would be a very favourable product interchange between ICE and aluminium processors, which would improve the viability of both products.

Action Raising of private capital (if possible Scottish) was in hand. (Mr Thomson and Mr Robertson).'

"From the above minute it appears that the Highlands and Islands Development Board have decided to sink or swim with their part-time member Mr Frank Thomson. Not only have they paid large sums of money on studies to the benefit of Invergordon Chemical Enterprises; not only have they paid all the expenses of the trip to the States (and Mr Thomson charged them £21/12/- for one night spent in Room 514 of Fortes Airport Hotel on 22nd December before he left); not only have they admitted in their minutes that Mr Thomson is negotiating privately, and not on behalf of the Board; further they are even prepared to take over land which is proving an embarrassment to him when he cannot pay £15,000 he owes; and, even more important, they are leaving the raising of private capital not to him alone but to him and Mr Robertson. It is most unlikely that Mr Thomson can raise £15,000,000, when he is persona non grata in the city after being sacked by Mr Max Rayne. It can be seen that at the meeting of Kincraig Farmers in January, 1967 he could not even find £15,000. He is already indebted to the Board £23,500 and has been paid grants of £1,500. He is still trying to get Board money to save Ross-Shire Engineering which has lost £12,000 this year and must be insolvent. But the Board have burnt their boats so there is no escape – they must by hook or crook raise British money to match the money Occidental are to put up."